Statements and Reflections: A Process in Philosophical Discourse

Statements and Reflections: A Process in Philosophical Discourse

By

David Lloyd Briscoe, Ph.D.

E-BookTime, LLC
Montgomery, Alabama

Statements and Reflections:
A Process in Philosophical Discourse

Library of Congress Control Number: 2012901404

ISBN: 978-1-60862-369-3

First Edition
Published January 2012
E-BookTime, LLC
6598 Pumpkin Road
Montgomery, AL 36108
www.e-booktime.com

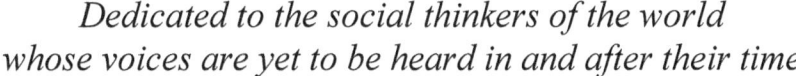

*Dedicated to the social thinkers of the world
whose voices are yet to be heard in and after their time*

Foreword

Statements and Reflections: A Process in Philosophical Discourse is a collection of statements generated over a period of several decades. All have come about as a result of my life experiences. The longer we live, the more opportunities we have to make a positive difference in ourselves as well as others.

David L. Briscoe, Ph.D.

"The difficult decisions we make are often the foundation from which character is forged"

"Calm yourselves by remembering your purpose; and energize yourselves with your destiny in mind"

"Every man is an example for another to follow"

"Life is surviving – emotionally, psychologically, and spiritually"

"Maturity is not allowing immaturity to take up residence in your life"

"Aspire to achieve that which is attainable"

"Maturity is living a simple life and becoming less burdened with the demands of social conformity"

"Submission to some aspects of social conformity is not a great credo"

"Racism is an evil, regardless of who the racist is!"

"Life is equally full of pain as gain and should be regarded as such"

"Life is not a piece of chocolate, nor is it a lemon. It is mostly what you forge, less that in which we have no control"

"I am my brother's keeper as long as he allows me the privilege"

"Racism and other forms of hatred are opportunities for you to let your light shine"

"Let your light shine, its radiance has unknown effects"

"It is amazing how one small light can lighten the darkest darkness"

"Never forget, there is a difference between light and darkness! Sometimes we dwell in darkness so long that we believe it to be light"

"Often times we internalize darkness to such a degree that we view it as light and light as darkness"

"Reach for the light; move towards the light; embrace the light; and live in the light"

"As we move from darkness to light, we begin to realize just how dark the night has become"

"What a breath of fresh air to discover that light has been there all along awaiting our discovery"

"Many have traveled the river unknown, few have returned"

"The reek of death permeates those who stare it in the face"

"The path to spiritual enlightenment is a consistent process of reducing oneself to selflessness in exchange for a true self"

"My eyes have indeed seen the coming of the Lord"

"Somewhere I lost confidence in what I thought mattered most, only to realize that it doesn't matter at all"

"The writer never stops writing even when the mechanics of the process is dead"

"Seize the moment lest you forget it"

"Asking God for answers might be the beginning of how to ask"

"Never expect that which has been established to become so easily uprooted"

"Man is consciously creating his present and future"

"What I have learned through the years is reality long forgotten"

"Every man should leave such a legacy that even an evil man would ponder with sincerity and contemplate emulating"

"Life is not only about living, but dying to life, resurrection, and rebirth"

"In a time distant or near, recognition is awaiting those whose deeds have been HOPE to a dying humanity"

"Long before the winter of life is complete, anticipate the genesis of spring with a bang!"

"Life is a series of seasons, ever the same, yet forever changing"

"Knowing the truth, yet buffeted by darkness makes for conflicting bedfellows"

"Seeking for the sake of ego never leaves it satisfied. It is an ever expanding abyss that is cancerous throughout eternity"

"Traveling an unknown path without some indication of the journey's end results in pain waiting to occur"

"Unknown paths do lead somewhere – unknown"

"The road less traveled is often the hardest and most loneliest, but the most satisfying"

"A man's life consists of what he has experienced, not what he has achieved"

"The risk of achieving at the risk of pain is self-agony"

"Dead history is social life once in existence but long since forgotten"

"If you are aware of your weaknesses, then you are in a good position to overcome your weaknesses"

"Positive sanctions in the form of awards and accolades are a small measure of a man's life and should be seen as such"

"Let the performance of service be a reminder of past blessings"

"The view of what one has is least in comparison to what one is"

"More is the impression of who one is if what is preached is practical."

"Consider flexibility in thought as opposed to rigidity"

"As one matures, so does his thinking about phenomena. Even if it takes a life time"

"Mental torment is the consequences of pondering the measures by which one might be evaluated"

"The attainment of each laurel wreath should be remembered as unique in and of itself, and not to be compared with another or ranked in a hierarchy"

"The allegiance to material is bondage to folly"

"Physical death is the consequence of social living"

"Dying never begins momentarily since it is a lifelong perpetual process"

"Find truth, live truth; and be truthful"

"I miss those not seen and those not heard"

"The eagle soars high and the morning sun shines bright. I am in my place and the place is within its context waiting for my reaction"

"Godly blessings bring godly character, and godly character brings about a godly destiny"

"Godly character is evident when you deny yourself of worldly indulgencies"

"Godly character is a process, created one experience at a time, regardless of frequency and intensity"

"When you give hope, you give an essence of LIFE that benefits both the giver and the receiver"

"The pathway to spiritual maturity is relative to an individual's willingness to walk the path to glory"

"Reality is a relative issue. An issue subject to an individual's interpretation and ability to see indiscriminately"

"Grow me and withdraw not your hand. Love me unconditionally and I will replicate the process"

"It seems as if I have traversed a million miles; witnessed a billion sunrises and sunsets; and prayed a trillion prayers"

"The morning seems brighter, and midnight, a hallmark for ending, and the beginning of another"

"Life is forever ongoing, always in balance, and always complete"

"When people hinder you in the achievement of your goals, or become attitudinal toward you about having achieved your goals, love them all the more!"

"My wish is for all people to be at peace within themselves. This would make for a saner and less troubled world"

"Reality is more than what we are able to see or touch, but also what we hold in our hearts"

"There are many places we choose not to return, as there are many such people"

"We give our best for a cause in hopes that it's good enough to inspire others to better living"

"Ignore not the righteous path made known to you"

"Be less concerned with what an individual wears on his face, and more concerned with what he holds in his heart"

"Inspiration does come, although the time, place, and situation can be most unusual"

"Be less taken with the outer and more so with the inner, provided that what's inside suits your taste"

"The least well known often puzzles those who have been groomed to be socialites"

"The path to pleasing others takes its toll, resulting in a change of pace and a reverberation of the soul"

"May God's mercy be on those who have closed their eyes by their own hand?"

"Lacking in what you need is a time to question if you really need it"

"Always remember that the mind and the heart are two separate phenomenons"

"The mind forgets, but the heart remembers"

"There comes a time when all else is isolated from who you really are"

"If you remain in unhealthy relationships, then always expect your peace to be subject to disharmony"

"There is a personal and collective price to pay for peace"

"Peace is most relevant to its cost, and is on a continuum to a lesser or greater extent"

"The progression to peace is not always nonlinear, but a series of lines, angles, and geometric figures"

"Relinquish not your peace to anyone, to anything, and to any cause less you are willing to be destroyed"

"Longing for that special one is most painful, especially when they exist in the same space"

"Only you can assist yourself through some things, and only God can bring you through all things. Oh! The limitations of the mind"

"There is no need to sit and cry about some situation. However, there is the need to move into action"

"There is a point beyond your grip to return"

"Some travel different paths, but face similar challenges"

"We all might see the coming of the Lord in many different forms"

"The process to destiny is never as significant as the final destination"

"The desire is to make your life count as none other. Therefore, you will always be competing with yourself to the very end"

"In many instances, some people have more courage than brains regarding some situations and circumstances"

"Man is often the better when he seeks wise counsel from the truly wise"

"The man who provides wise counsel is often the better for having done so"

"Acts of apology are the foundation upon which self respect is born"

"It's not always the indigent who falls to his knees and utters prayers for deliverance"

"Hurrying the day is the rushing of time; and the rushing of time is the rushing of life; and the rushing of life is the rushing to death"

"Better to suffer for righteousness than to enjoy pleasures in which carries a throne"

"Resist the urge to become as others wish you to become"

"Every predicament is an opportunity in masquerade"

"There is an immense outlay for enlightenment and an even greater one for illiteracy"

"It is not the symbolic form that holds a man's vigor but the radiance of spirit embodied in its significance"

"If in the Christian perspective one internalizes who he is, then any other expression becomes second place, and the crave to consummate sociable stations in life becomes pithy, and the tussle of earthly life more bearable."

"There is perpetually grace in suffering whether for the sake of righteousness or refraining from unrighteousness"

"Sometimes no one believes you; no one knows you; and no one will offer a helping hand"

"Marital exhilaration is never fathomed for the many that rise in astonishment awaiting its brilliance"

"All one can do in a solitary union is to take his marriage vows earnestly"

"Seldom does anyone discern the anguish of those with the enormous smile"

"As I near the end and reflect upon the journey, I long for more, yet not knowing for how much or for how less"

"Awareness of the meaning of one's achievement is most worthy and noble"

"Look in the mirror and see how much life is left, or better yet, how much life has evaporated since yesterday"

"As you ripen, matters once held paramount suddenly lose its appeal into a state of nothingness"

"Mortality is transitory, abiding between two antithetical ultimates – birth and extinction"

"If what you are; and if what you are about is not in line with God, then you are not about your father's business"

"Hello cherished comrade; I must do whatever to apprise you of truth, only to my realization that you must enter this realm alone"

"The footpath of life often becomes a thoroughfare and the thoroughfare a step"

"Alone on life's journey is not an indication of loneliness, but a sign of the few in pursuit of the journey"

"Adversities, sufferings, and sorrows are all fragments of life's vibrant birth pains"

"Maturity is consenting to release the seemingly important"

"The genuinely conduct of existing will invariably present many tribulations"

"Any thing can befall a man at any given time. However, imprudent resolutions augment the chances of cataclysm"

"The counting of blessings gives insufficient leeway for the blues"

"Edicts are decreed, altered, and disintegrated by those empowered at a given point in time; therefore such canons are germane to the notions of the empowered"

"Life is needed not at the risk of death; however, life is the genesis to death as death is the genesis to life"

"Sometimes it is not what turns us on that's evocative, but what doesn't turn us on"

"Unlawful love is unholy and unholy love is death to the lovers"

"Man's greatest adversaries are: the self, the world, and the devil"

"A man without peace is a man without LIFE"

"Man is the editor of his biography and often its principal witness"

"Before blaming a man for my mishaps, I must first examine my soul in hopes of finding it blameless"

"The scales covering a man's eyes are sealed with glue which only time can unseal"

"Much of LIFE is in the choices made concerning it"

"As man ascends the spiritual spiral, he often looks from whence he came with surprise and astonishment"

"A man's soul is calm only when it is holy"

"Man often builds his tomb by the ways in which he chooses to live his life"

"The simple man is often more enlightened than we give credit, and the much acclaimed is often more ignorant than we anticipated."

"Education is the accrual of human ideas which in many respects are not relevant to LIFE"

"Every day is a day of spiritual warfare and man's soul is the warrior who fights relentlessly in a lump of clay"

"One attempt to manipulate another is to undermine his self-confidence"

"People think they know each other, only to discern that no person is truly known. Who knows the mind of another?"

"Life is a passageway that each person must pass, usually by alone"

"It is astonishing how life's excursions are a combination of rain and sunshine. And more often than not, we are the mastermind of the rain and the sunshine"

"You may take away what I have but never who I am"

"It is who I am that will win the day and never what I have"

"To do that which is righteous is the best thing a person can do. No one said the path is easy, or the desire is overwhelming"

"If you are using drugs while attending school, stop and think that what you are trying to perfect, you are in the process of destroying"

"Sometimes you must stop, evaluate your life, and make choices as how to best handle the problems you have been avoiding"

"Have you asked yourself lately what direction your life is heading?"

"Ask yourself if the manner in which you are living your life is helping or hindering your spiritual growth"

"Do right because it is right"

"It only takes a few minutes to begin a lifelong habit. Be careful what you do in the next few minutes"

"Sooner or later we must look our problems straight in the face"

"Doing right is not easy, it's often difficult. Just remember, if there is no pain, usually there is no gain."

"Understanding is one of the greatest attributes in the world"

"Minority status is another opportunity to express love to a color conscious society"

"Always let your light shine, maybe it will guide some lost soul from a state of obscurity"

"There is enough darkness in the world. Consider not adding to it"

"The more light there is, the more it radiates. Many lights, one great FIRE"

"Blackness is showing the world that you have backbone to withstand in a hostile society"

"There are some things only time can teach you; therefore time is your teacher"

"Mind over matter? Better said, heart over matter"

"The right road is always a difficult one"

"Sin weakens the strong man. It never leaves him as he once was. It takes something away that must be restored"

"The breath of LIFE is not always physical, and the sting of death is not always the obvious"

"Discipline is a hard master"

"A disciplined life is a conquered one"

"Every man will fight his share of life's battles. There are no exceptions. How man emerges from battle depends upon his preparation, skill at fighting, and spiritual acumen"

"The worse type of battle is mental whose host wears the mask of happiness and the heart of the dead"

"One cannot always prepare in advance for everything that comes upon him"

"Disappointments can be a friend or an enemy. They come in many forms, and are spontaneous to say the least"

"With each passing day, I am nearer to my end in this dimension, yet closer to a state of ecstasy"

"Birth and death are common features to man's existence. For within man, many births and deaths take place over time"

"Don't risk your joy, peace, and contentment over uncertainties"

"When dealing with negative emotions, expect miracles of vast dimensions"

"You may not have the moon or the stars, but you can have joy, peace, and contentment concerning the moon and the stars. Such attributes are more significant and more meaningful than you know"

"Your righteousness will make you whole"

"Sin is an agent whose purpose is to disorganize and to destroy"

"There is a joy that comes from knowing that you are at least attempting to live a righteous life"

"Discipline is often a hard but needed friend"

"Going HOME might be as easy as waking up"

"The greatest man is one who is spiritually developed"

"Everything is in the process of decadence"

"Time keeps no watch over itself"

"Never allow another person the privilege to control your body, mind, or spirit. If so, the consequences are often grave from which you might never recover"

"Power is not only an attribute of the strong but also of the weak"

"Sin separates God from man"

"Sin is darkness and no light can be found in it"

"The volume of sin can overcome too little light"

"The smallest light has the most impact in the darkest night"

"The state of darkness prevents seeing reality clearly"

"Living a righteous life does not imply freedom from temptation. As a matter of fact, for the righteous, temptation seems to be everywhere all the more, attempting to consume the very life of the individual"

"Spiritual growth will often not grow in proportion to social progress"

"Many battles are fought in the body and perhaps more so in the mind"

"The body is often slave to the mind"

"The mind is fragile and should be regarded with much care"

"War is common to man whether it is of a physical or mental nature"

"War always means death and victory on behalf of someone or some nation"

"Spiritual maturity is the foundation for battle"

"Righteousness is always the reason for further righteousness"

"Applying righteousness is not a reason to inflict punishment on the righteous"

"Sometimes it's not how long you remain in a location, but how effective you are while you're there"

"The distinguished scholar seldom gets recognized"

"Distinguished persons are present in all walks of life and in all social positions, whether they are rich or poor, or regardless of the color variable"

"A price can never be assigned to joy, peace, and contentment"

"What price would some people pay for peace of mind?"

"What is contentment? And what is the value of it"

"The best thing of value is that which nothing can destroy"

"Spiritual maturity is the ultimate by which nothing can be measured or evaluated"

"Man judges the outer man; God judges the heart"

"Spiritual reality is an awesome experience like none other!"

"Everything is resolved to spiritual enlightenment"

"It is gratifying to focus upon the experiences leading to an achievement rather than the achievement itself. Such a process is a mental or spiritual endeavor that cannot be taken from you or destroyed"

"Life goes on and in the process comes its share of joy, pain, and heartbreak – so is life"

"Living is what you make it; LIFE is partly the culmination of living"

"You will learn of me best when I no longer exist. After all, you will have all the time in the world to miss me. Hardly do we miss another without thinking of them in depth and all other aspects"

"Love me genuinely while you have the opportunity, and kiss me tenderly before the dawn"

"Oftentimes we grow from sorrows, oftentimes we die from it"

"Heart attacks are more than a physical phenomenon, they are spiritual as well"

"Love does not always love back. Sometimes it remains a neutral force, perhaps forever"

"If you had the power to resurrect a lost love, would you do so?"

"A hurting heart may never heal, and a dying heart may never die"

"A strong man has his weaknesses; and a weak man his strengths"

"I am unable to be everything to all people"

"Some things are obvious, yet other things remain a mystery"

"Take me to another place where the context is different, yet somewhat familiar"

"On the one hand I wish to see you, and on the other I am scared to death. Oh! What a terrible fix to be in"

"At one time or another, every man stands tall on his own soap box"

"Death is the release of the soul by which LIFE is now everlasting for evermore"

"Happiness as often defined as to what's happening in one's environment must not be thought of as true happiness which is a permanent state of being"

"Man is eternally connected, if not by a spiritual consciousness but by the earth from whence he came. Therefore, we are brothers and sisters from earth's dusty domain. Forever to return back to it without our permission"

"Sometimes love can be withheld from another too long. However, if we have true love for another, why then would one withhold that what seems to be a natural process"

"Loving involves the use of both body and mind. This process seems simpler than complex, but more complex than simple"

"The loneliest man is one who knows that he is truly alone"

"Later might mean better"

"Greatness is determined through the realization of how little one needs to be so great"

"Man tends to fill his life with things that are forever becoming transparent"

"Some people run towards mountains and giants, others run frantically from them"

"Some desire to remain lost while others are crying out to be found"

"If you think you have little, then lose it and then reevaluate your situation"

"It's not a crime or sin to be happy with the simple things of life"

"Some have run a thousand miles, and have no idea where they have been or where they are going"

"I am an engine pulling the cars of life, while at other times; I am the caboose providing guidance from the rear"

"Help me please to make a better world, or get out of my path and I will do it alone"

"Some have truly seen the coming of the Lord!"

"All love is not true, therefore love in its varied forms need to be tested to ascertain if it's worth its salt"

"Truth forces one to examine one's lifestyle"

"Truth is comparable to light, and where there is light, darkness cannot be found but in memory"

"Failing to receive some accolade can be as positively intoxicating as receiving it in form"

"What an honor when you know you are living a righteous life before almighty God"

"Accepting the truth forces one to consider applying the truth"

"Knowing the truth and failing to submit to it is utter agony"

"When God blesses you with little, always regard it as much!"

"Look only to God for your rewards instead of man who often than not gives you a thorn"

"Simplicity is a state of mind as well as a state of being happy with little"

"There is much joy, peace, and a sense of accomplishment upon realizing the consequences of simplicity"

"There tends to be much joy and peace as a person moves into the realm of simplicity. The entire process is based on time and is often the result of freeing oneself from that which restrains"

"The objective is always to move from a life of complications to one of simplicity"

"God truly observes the good that we do and He alone will reward us accordingly"

"Walk in love; rejoice always; in everything gives thanks; fear not, only believe; ask and you shall receive; and forgive, and you shall be forgiven"

"Nothing is as significant and productive than acquiring the WORD and making it a part of you"

"Your strength lies in your humility"

"He sent his WORD into a dying world to save it from destruction; some freely received it while others freely disregarded it"

"Choose not to partake in situations that will become the basis for your demise"

"Man more often than not holds the keys to heaven and hell. The keys are the choices he makes about the destination that is before him"

"Life without purpose is compared to a cylinder without contents – empty"

"Life is full of boxes, some big, some small, some beautiful, some ugly, some enticing, others enchanting, yet they all share the same objective – to hold that which has been enclosed"

"Get out of the box or you will remain boxed!"

"The portrait of life is always how you live it, and each stroke of the brush is in itself the years of anguish and toil that often gives life its precious meaning!"

"The scroll of life is mostly what you choose and the deeds that follow thereafter"

"Hear you, hear ye, my life is a testament of my thoughts and a reflection of my choices"

"Heartbreak is the clay of life by which we are molded in stature and purified into righteous decency for a rendez-vous with the Holy One"

"Life is a series of experiences that produce many dimen-sions of mind, heart, and soul"

"Life is a test of tests that we rarely pass with the lowest score"

"As time runs its course, I am sure that my end is nearer than yesterday"

"As a traveler beyond the half century mark, I am able to see life better than before, and care less about the mundane things of life"

"I envy no man, but wonder about each one"

"As knowledge increases, so does the ability of the prudent man to separate the wheat from the chaff"

"The tests of life are often many, thus becoming an arena of opportunities that we usually fail to take full advantage"

"Man ALONE is a lonely being, even in the company of hundreds, perhaps thousands"

"The company of the lonely is not always the salve that eases the pains of the heart"

"Some of us simply want to show others love and kindness and send them on their way. Funny isn't it. That's all [LOVE] some people need"

"Why does it take humans a life time to learn how to LIVE as opposed to how to earn a living?"

"Living can be as sweet or as sour as we choose. The art is in the choosing!"

"So much of life is learning how to live it, and how to maintain its luster"

"Don't be fooled by the abilities of the ordinary man, and disappointed by those who claim to know it all"

"What does the heart say to itself, what does it say when it's almost broken, and what does it say when death is its captive. Does it know! Does it know?"

"Reality is more than what you see and touch, it all that we deem part of us"

"What is real to one person might not be so to another, therefore we second guess each other as to his sanity or insanity"

"Life has a way of breaking even the strongest man who has never learned to live it"

"Living life is the act of mere existence until LIFE emerges from the shadow of hell"

"LIFE is the ultimate goal of those who breathe without reservation"

"As strength is power to the body, so is spiritual maturity food for the soul"

"Life does not give you all you need, nor does it give you all that you want. Instead, life gives, and it's up to you to decide how best to deal with what is given"

"Beginning again is not always easy, but it is a start, a potential for something new, something positive"

"Negative memories will eventually resurface. It's probably best to give them little, if any attention"

"A good role model is not enough; a person needs to be a Godly one"

"Whatever you do in life, make sure you are on a Godly path and not just on any old path"

"Wake up from your natural moment of slumber to catch a fleeing glimpse of reality"

"Everything is a process experienced by each person to a greater or lesser degree"

"Discipline yourself into making every moment count. Regret serves no genuine purpose and is an agent of degradation"

"Life is full of decisions that have to be made, and your earthly and eternal destiny's depend on them"

"Do good to all and ALL will be the consequences"

"We easily tire of routines after a period of time. Make the attempt to diversify the routines and life will probably be better and more enjoyable"

"A kind word spoken gives life to the bones and substance to the act of living"

"Never turn your back on the individual who brings you a cup of water"

"Gems of gold are forever around you, so are the thrones too"

"The acid test of the situation is coming into the realization that what you thought to be a big deal is really nothing at all"

"Low level living brings about low level results, if any"

"Low level living brings high level consequences"

"Recognize the trappings of bondage"

"The Christian should encourage, comfort, and urge other Christians to live worthy of the cross"

"Those we serve become our joy and our glory"

"We are too quick to point out what we have achieved in the natural order, but often fail to even hint of what we have amassed in the spiritual realm. Could it be that the accomplishments of the world are deemed more important? Or, could it be that we haven't any spiritual achievements to boast about?"

"The spiritual realm is a reality that supersedes the natural world in quality, substance, and time"

"The natural world is a laboratory that offers the individual hope through expression in a transient context that is unreal"

"There is more power and character in saying no than when saying yes, especially when motives are unclear or absent"

"Wisdom is advancing to a level that you will never completely know and that which you already know is subject to scrutiny and vague interpretation"

"Time is of the moment and is forever running its course"

"It's a marvelous thing to reflect on time, especially time well spent. But don't spend too much time in the reflective process because life is more than a reflection"

"Study the Book of Life; more importantly, live it"

"The knowledge of truth comes when the effort to secure it is manifested"

"Again and again I exclaim, live that which has been bestowed instead of wearing it out"

"The greatest endeavor is assisting in the redemption of mankind"

"You can experience victory in the midst of the storm"

"Even when you think that no one knows or understand your plight, there is ONE who knows and beyond measure understands"

"There is true peace that transcends what we consciously know as peace"

"The real Christian must emerge from the world or perish within it and lose all hope for eternal life"

"When one fails to do his best, he is forever reminded of it"

"Along the path of time, the man of insight catches a glimpse of how short physical life really is"

"Many a man have fought a good fight, but few have kept the faith"

"The Christian life is a disciplined one"

"Joy always comes when you sincerely give from the heart"

"Much of what you have will never be known to the many"

"Blessings are often thought of in physical forms and not in spiritual ones"

"Think about the spiritual essence as embodied in a thing"

"Sometimes, the physical manifestation of matter does not imply spiritual reality."

"Assisting people in reaching their goals and objectives is just as meaningful as achieving them yourself"

"Just as one has high moments, the low moments will come too"

"Some people receive the prize; others receive the spirit of it"

"The spirit of a thing is just as real as the thing itself"

"Be happy and glad that some things you desired at one point in life never became so"

"Some people and events you never get over. Instead you carry the memory afresh"

"Give not into the ways of the world lest you risk being a victim of it"

"The social system has ways of developing you, and ways of destroying you as well. Therefore you are the master, based upon the choices you give to the system"

"LIFE leads you beyond life, and the acceptance of its consequences is most sweet"

"What was once thought to be grandiose is now reduced to rubble"

"When you spend time in the WORD you are never the same!"

"I am better through self discipline and the worst without it"

"The world is constantly spinning, and if one is not careful, he will spin with it to a point of no control"

"Again, take my hand and learn from me, as I take yours"

"Many have not been to the mountaintop and few to the valley below"

"Joy comes when we observe how much we have become like Christ and less like the world"

"Feelings have nothing to do with truth, but the discovery of truth is experienced with awesome feelings"

"Trouble can be candy-coated, so beware"

"The experience of negative pleasures certainly has it consequences"

"Integrity is what you have after withstanding the tests of time"

"In time, the things you thought were so important have now taken on minuscule meaning"

"Sometimes there is much difficulty in our search for comfort in the middle of a tragedy. Yet, the difficulty does not mean that solace is not there awaiting our discovery"

"Always keep your focus on God through His Son Jesus Christ lest we forget"

"Sometimes you must stir yourself to the call for action"

"When feeling down and rejected, focus on your purpose in life. If your purpose is true, the probability of feeling better is more likely to occur"

"Life will not always present to you a thorn, or a silver platter. Most often it's a combination of both"

"Keep your focus on the higher calling. Keep the vision in plain sight"

"Never think I will not love you for the honest utterance of the lips"

"Somehow, the aura of the soul speaks much louder in silence than words spoken with the softest lips"

"My heart is aching, but a renewed spirit is emerging"

"There is a place awaiting my arrival, and a place from whence I must leave"

"I desire to give of myself"

"Each day is another landmark that I will never witness again in passing"

"When encouragement from significant others is not forthcoming, then it must be sought from another source. Ponder well the source as if your very life depended upon it"

"Encourage everyone to develop a living philosophy and to set realistic goals consistent with it"

"Live life in a manner that amazes those who doubt you and to those who hold you up before the light"

"Live life to your own astonishment! Such frame of reference sets the platform by which bigger dreams are acted out on the stage of life"

"Make life count while you may, for each new day brings you closer to an ending, yet, to a new beginning"

"Goal setting should incorporate all the attributes relative to LIFE"

"The flesh enhances thinking, and too much thinking produces fleshly actions. Beware of what you think"

"Fear in some aspects can be traced to our giving too much attention to the flesh"

"Every thought that enters the mind does not have to dwell there"

"Negative situations are actually gems in the sand awaiting your discovery"

"Give no one the ammunition to an already smoking gun"

"When evidence of my presence no longer exists...
and the conversation about me is no longer uttered....
The fact is: I was here"

"Some things you must give up in order to gain something more"

"Holding on to death is a good sign that you don't know the difference between LIFE and death"

"Put LIFE not in jeopardy for the sake of life's temptations"

"The highest priority is living righteously before almighty God, and because of this, some paths must not be crossed and some bridges must not be burned"

"Strongholds in an individual's life are comparable to a completely dark room in which there is no light. As long as darkness fills the room, LIGHT cannot enter. Somehow, in our darkest hour, we must make a way for LIGHT to find its way. Once there, it has the potential to eradicate the darkness, one second at a time"

"When you react to who you really are, you then fail to react in the same manner as to who others thought you were"

"Don't give LIFE up so easily. As a matter of fact, never give it up at all!"

"Choose not to partake in any situation that becomes the basis for your demise"

"It's no surprise that the individual is tempted. This is a natural process and should be expected, but the enlightened person should have the character and spiritual insight to put this spiritual phenomenon in the proper context within an instance without debate or moments of reflection"

"Consequences follow all actions, and we are the better if we concentrate long and hard on both"

"I have been of one nature, and now I am in the process of another from which the former has no roots"

"In one manner or another, the individual has his audience to cheer either way for his ascendancy or for his imprisonment."

"Count all your experiences as blessings, whether you evaluate them as good, bad, or in-between"

"Opportunities come in many forms, and disguises."

"Dare to analyze a negative situation for the good that lies within"

"Life is a journey comprised of second by second experiences that shape and redefine our destiny"

"Never shelve a Bible"

"Marriage without intimacy is compared to a bag without a bottom"

"Intimacy in a marriage is not always present at the time of marriage, but the potential for its birth should be a desired effect"

"Never express too much regarding any phenomenon. Because much of what is expressed might not be true, even if you claim to be an expert"

"Silence is really a golden experience. It allows us the time to process what others declare, and the opportunity to reflect on our state of being"

"There are some things that should never be uttered; others things that should be considered; and yet other things we take to the grave"

"Seek the moment of silence and see what discovery waits. Many people are challenged to disengage the mouth and the body from action"

"Sad is the day when the realization comes that nothing is between those who dreamed of having so much, but have so little"

"There are too many definitions and interpretations of true love, and many variations in existence"

"Living to achieve LIFE is life at its best, and living without such a purpose is ultimately life at its worst"

"There are many deaths as well as many resurrections. Are you dead, or have you been resurrected?"

"Say little about what you know, and listen more than you speak. Everyone will probably be better off"

"Guard well your lips and much more your heart"

"True love can never be coerced on another; neither can it be illuminated for those who choose not to receive it"

"Tears alone can comfort little, but there is a cleansing effect for those who are able to cry"

"Living to achieve LIFE is life in abundance"

"There are many deaths as well as many resurrections"

"Physical death is the ultimate of dying and the consequences of this phenomenon is LIFE everlasting for those prepared to accept it"

"Say less than what you know, and listen more to what is spoken"

"Guard well your lips"

"Discipline is a hard master from which the essence of LIFE is forged"

"To engage at the risk of death is worthy of reconsideration"

"A personal philosophy is a beacon of light that becomes the guiding force in all endeavors"

"When your world seems so complex and chaotic, clear the path for that inspiration of light"

"Time is a headstone to a greater or lesser degree"

"As you move from place to place, and from time to time, my pray is that everything is as you desire it to be"

"Happy is the man who leaves a legacy of peace"

"Who knows the mind of another person? After all, what he thinks is what he thinks"

"Develop a philosophy, manage your time and resources, speak the truth, give to others and watch the grass grow green and the thorns wilt and die"

"Whatever happens, we will be better for it"

"Respond not to the world as it responds to you"

"Spiritual reality and maturity is a higher state of consciousness"

"Spiritual consciousness or maturity is the highest endeavor that one can achieve and nothing can match it"

"Meaning is a spiritual activity"

"Think beyond or outside the natural world and see aspects of a world unknown to mortal man"

"A simple soul; yet making a dynamic impact on humanity"

"Be careful in expressing your honesty, there are those who might not be spiritually mature to handle such an expression"

"Many followers of time have regarded journaling as a squander of time, mental energy, and acumen. Some might ponder why an individual would put pen to paper about his ideas. A generalization is posited that such an endeavor affords the author to chronicle his ideas and frames of reference overtime for others to ruminate and consider"

"There is never an escaping from ourselves, even for a short period of time. We must come back to ourselves and face the reality of our living on the pathway to our dying"

"I would rather wrestle against committing an act than to commit the act and wrestle with why I committed it"

"Battling against forces is common to man. There seems to be little escape from this perpetual warfare"

"Amidst the toils and snares of life, there is a sense of accomplishment in overcoming. This alone gives meaning to life and a better understanding of the life process"

"Some of us never escape nor overcome our trials and tribulations. Instead, they become part of us. They venture the path of life with us, and end with us in the state of death"

"Observe situations for what they are and declare whether you responded to them in an appropriate manner"

"Situations in and of themselves don't cause the dilemmas of life, but our retort to them is the causal factor to be reckoned with"

"SPIRIT over matter is the objective, rather than mind over matter. Mind is a natural consequence of profane reality, whereas SPIRIT is an outer-world phenomenon embracing the spiritual world, thus controlling the natural world"

"The essence of man is to deal with social phenomena from a spiritual basis. Spirituality is in itself a process based on time and events. It's not achieved all at once. It often comes about in gradual steps in its own way. Man can never hurry that which he has no control. And that which he has no control is always the master of all"

"Man's objective should be to achieve meaning from his life experiences. Every experience can be one of profound meaning if we choose to make it so"

"Man's search for meaning is not through the acquisition of things"

"Always think before you commit an action. In doing so, the consequences might be better"

"When feeling bad or sad, just count your blessings. Surely, there is one or a thousand blessings brought to mind that will brighten your day and give you hope for a better tomorrow"

"Count it a blessing every time someone offers a helping hand or a word of encouragement"

"Never feel guilty about what is natural and what appears as common sense"

"You can never be something that you're not on the inside. There is little room for pretending to be somebody else!!!!!"

"So much I thought I knew about everything, only to disclose that I know very little about anything"

"I am convinced that each of us must gaze into the mirror of life and expose the thousands of forces by which we are both judge and jury"

"There has never been or will be any position higher or more ultimate than that of a child of God. All the toil and effort to achieve the so-called ultimate will end in one never achieving it. However, internalizing who you truly are will out-satisfy any desire of the social world"

"We wish to make the world better for those we love more than anyone else"

"As we truly love those we love, we truly suffer too on their behalf, because we truly love those we love"

"We learn over time what true love is really about, and its substance is infinite and without form"

"Physical love is a manifestation of both heart and the mind, and who is to say more than those who give and from those who receive it"

"Living life is an endowment and a delight, all wrapped into one universe"

"Everyone will not see your love if they have not the eyes to see, or the ears to hear, or the capacity to grasp its fundamental nature"

"Some doors we close and others are closed for us against our wills"

"Once the door to a situation is closed, consider having it sealed as well"

"Love cannot be ordered around; it can only be what it is. It has its own momentum, style, way, and eventually its own death."

"Look, open your mind and heart and see my love as freely yours. It is yours to have and to cherish as long as you freely receive it"

"We love and love; hoping that what we offer to another is enough. Sometimes, it rarely is, but it's all we have"

"Much of what is declared as love is not love at all. Instead, it is a mere delusion of what we wish it to be"

"All we can do is show our love for another person, the rest is up to them"

"We make no one love us. It's either there within them or not"

"Man digs the pit that eventually swallows him"

"The natural mind is at odds with the slightest hint of reformation"

"As the natural gives sway to the spiritual, it is as though the natural has lost part of itself and feels strange and alien"

"Change is not always easy in many situations, and some situations are less amenable to change than others"

"Change often rocks our world, and our world is a change agent within itself"

"Take notice of the changes you have gone through; the changes you are experiencing; the changes that have taken your breath way; and the imposing changes that will contribute to your eternal destiny"

"We stand to provide testimonies of the changes in our lives, and whether we have persevered or failed, the changes have made their impact on us in some manner"

"Flee evil as to make room for the presence of good"

"Maintain your spiritual focus and your spiritual insight will sustain you when all else fails, especially when there is no shoulder cry on and no pillow to rest your weary head"

"The attributes of greatness are: patience, steadfastness, and self control"

"When you have IT within, then there is nothing you need from without"

"Life is a process of discovering who we really are, although we fight living without embracing the moments"

"A time is emerging upon life's journey, slowly, but surely time will win this battle, however, LIFE will prove the victor"

"Live unto yourself and unfold like the lotus"

"Observe all trials and tribulations as challenges, and challenges as opportunities; and speak of such matters in such a manner"

"Life is forever challenging, complex, and yes, worth living"

"I am who I am. No more or less. I am simply who I am"

"Reality is both nonmaterial and material, be careful not to confuse the two"

"Regardless of whether you achieve the brass ring, this is no true indicator that others will regard you as worthy. Oftentimes, the attainment of some supreme prominence brings with it negative and unwanted behaviors from the very ones who claim to love us the most"

"Man should never allow things to define who he is. Instead, the definition of self should be based upon what man has becomes in the absence of material acquisition"

"Having done right against the forces to do wrong has made all the difference in the world"

"I continue to travel the path, knowing that by faith the journey will end"

"The way is easy but the realization is astounding"

"The traveler desires to quit, and at other times to persevere. Each accomplishment is a step in the right direction. Oh God! I am so tired!"

"My colleagues before me venture on their path. I envy their place, knowing that when I equal them, another dream will befall me"

"You must remind yourself daily that you did the right thing regarding situations that were out of your control"

"The right thing to do is not always the easiest, neither is the wrong thing!"

"All that you have achieved in the natural realm are just things and no compelling evidence as to who you truly are. Who you truly are is beyond all measure of earthly success"

"True love never dies; however, it might be put on hold, or suspended for a season"

"Love! Oh love! Oh love! The magnitude of your power, the gentleness of your essence, the patience of your ways, and the pain is more than mortal man can bear. The desire to experience you is without bounds, the willingness to know you is forever on my lips and soul. And to love and not be loved is utter despair that the scales cannot balance nor can the heart forgive"

"Experiences are just as comparable as displaying a chest full of medals in appraising worth, competency, and well-being"

"The door opens, but only a certain type of individual walks through it"

"Life is about change and responding to life and change simultaneously"

"The time comes when changes in one's life produce defining moments in experiences of those changes"

"It's a good thing when changes are viewed as agents of the life process"

"As change agents, we consistently collide into the wrappings of other agents, thus declaring how their changes interface with our own"

"The realization of personal changes is a sobering experience as a grain of sand in the hour glass of time"

"Make friends with change because change is as pervasive as time"

"Fear not if you are not fully cognizant of the changes that have embraced your being"

"Never give another person the power to engage in recreating your heart"

"Life is not always easy. And it wasn't meant to be. Nor did anyone say it would be"

"Rolling with the punches and the tide does not always mean that you come out the victor"

"Be cognizant of your spiritual philosophy, as it will be a springboard to life and a fountain from which to drink"

"We tend to engage in events that have the potential of yielding the most rewards as well as the most meaning"

"One person receives the brass ring; another person receives a decoration of far less significance. The general idea accorded to each is less, equal, or more depending on the recipient's frame of reference"

"Be happy that you are freed from the trappings of the world by the Spirit of the universe"

"Bondage is a terrible master that absorbs the very life from that which it constricts"

"What a dilemma to experience when love says no to whom it loves"

"Love should allow the touch of satin and the comfort of an embrace"

"Lack of knowledge confines man's potential from becoming judicious"

"All that you are will sooner or later be revealed to an audience whose utterance of revelation will all too soon be forgotten"

"We are but a moment in the vast epoch of time, awaiting our eternal destiny"

"Greater honor comes to those who toil for the greater good"

"The ardent thinker takes a seat in the balcony of time and reflects upon where he's been and where he is likely to end his course"

"My wish for all mankind is that we live a life of peace, joy, and prosperity"

"Materialism gives way to more materialism, and the acquisition of such leads to the acquisition of such"

"Time has a way of revealing all things to the mind in lifelong increments. When the credits are given for such revelation, time in itself takes the credit"

"Insight into oneself is the beginning of true knowledge, but the realization is that the individual constantly looks within to understand"

"All that I am is small compared to all that I am becoming"

"So much to do; and so little, if any time to do it"

"The love that we give will unlikely be returned in proportion to which it was given"

"Some have so much love to give and so few who are willing to accept it"

"The yearning of others to give so much compassionate love can often leave the desired recipient speculating whether he or she is prepared to receive it"

"Some people long to search for what they have truly missed"

"No one can claim another's love if it's not yours to lay hold of"

"Love me as if there were no other, or free me as if I have been caged for an eternity"

"From a spiritual perspective, the individual has everything within to be successful"

"In Christ, I can be no more than I am"

"Blessings are to be exclaimed, and shared"

"Each blessing, whether spiritual or material, has its own special meaning, and should be regarded as such"

"My joy is not so much from desiring a thing as it is not being cognizant of having to have it"

"When you have internalized your blessings, there is little need to chase after windmills"

"The acquisition of the physical will never satisfy the craving of the soul"

"Be loving to all since we are confronted with challenges relative to human existence"

"I am unaware of all your challenges and the dynamics therein, but I am aware of a source that permeates all and all"

"Give of yourself as a conduit to alleviate the pain and suffering of others, and in return, you too will be healed"

"A thoughtful heart is a merry one, and a merry heart is a spring of joy from which everyone will stop and drink"

"Joy is a spiritual appetizer that becomes a full course meal"

"The few are often greater than the many, and the many are subject to the view of none"

"If you never seek, you usually never find"

"What you seek is usually what you find"

"Seek wise counsel from the wise and be yet wiser"

"Much of the world will watch you plummet, few, if any will endeavor to pick you up"

"The spirit of a servant must be sown in the days of our youth for an abundant return in the golden years"

"Old age should be an instant in time for gracious reflection on a life well spent"

"The golden years should be a season of joy, peace, and contentment, based upon the foundation of service to others"

"The objective of old age is never to arrive with decades of regrets
by which little can be done to eradicate them"

"The Holy writ is not to be read with aggression, but with the power and skill of an analytical investigator"

"Construct a reputation as a carpenter builds a house, one step at a time"

"Build a record as one builds a character. Both will coincide with the other, and happiness will be the reward"

"I am here and you are there, yet, for some strange reason, we share an affinity that only our souls can understand"

"Explore ways to be a support for others who are less fortunate than you"

"We might not have what we desired, or what we want, but for those of the faith, we have Jesus, and that makes all the eternal difference"

"Be a blessing wherever you pass through, whether to inhabitants, establishments, or any other social forms"

"In all things and in all ways, give thanks"

"Bring not rulings upon yourself because of your sensual decadence"

"Leading and preparing the way for Christ is the greatest achievement of all"

"Take your natural eyes off the situation and observe with a renewed vision"

"The Spirit of some things is not built by human hands"

"You might not be adorned with the laurel wreath, but that doesn't mean that you don't have facets of it"

"Give to the world a piece of righteousness and by such a seed is birthed into the conversion of many"

"A person has as much potential as a diamond in its luster"

"By words spoken or written, the universe was spawning as were great civilizations, past, present, and the future to come"

"Some people merely outgrow old habits, while other habits and attitudes remain with us to the end"

"There are some habits, beliefs, values, and attitudes that are too difficult for us to shake off. They remain with us as if they were our very breath"

"A person never truly knows the thoughts, feelings, or attitudes of another individual, regardless of how intense we endeavor to comprehend"

"We remain a mystery to others as well as to ourselves"

"We are constantly and consistently on a path called change, and the end thereof is not always predictable"

"How breathtaking it is to be participants in a world that's so dynamic and forever all-encompassing"

"We rarely see those who view our works"

"Life is a training ground to perfect entry into a sacred world"

"Where does man tread in a society that does not embrace him? Where does he hide when too many stones are hurled towards him? And how does he die when death has always engulfed him?"

"If people only knew the pain of another, and how well the bearer of pain bore their load, then rejoicing would surely come"

"Man often attempts to find meaning, purpose, and happiness in life apart from the SOURCE that really matters"

"Every man must walk a path, if not alone, but in his own shoes"

"Yesterday is tossed away with the wind and today is marred down in worry and concern about tomorrow"

"As yesterday is lost to history, so is the vision of the future without action"

"Mingle in the mist of the lost that they too might be found"

"If one accepts contentment, no longer will he seek outside for it"

"Very little truth is in man's standards, yet, standards are often internalized by man as truth by which civilizations have been judged and eliminated"

"Spiritual maturity must be applied to everyday living"

"Everyday living is harder to accomplish void of spiritual growth"

"You know who you are and what you have regardless if others give you what's due. Your understanding of this makes all the difference in the world"

"Spiritual maturity is thinking and behaving at a higher level"

"Physical death is the prelude to LIFE, and LIFE is the essence of everlasting LIFE"

"Degrees of spiritual maturity correlate to degrees of worldly separation"

"You have the revelations; write the WORD for all to see and know."

"Sexual exploitation of the self is a seed sown into the self that will bear fruit in proportion to the seed sown"

"Sexual abuse is a seed sown out of control"

"Sexual exploitation is both a consensual and a nonconsensual process"

"Live off the joy of what you have already experienced or achieved"

"If you have not achieved, then live off the joy of not feeling the need to achieve"

"Live off the joy of the experience of a thing and not the thing itself"

"Quick to death everything uttered"

"Say little, live long"

"Express nothing in private that you would not voice in public"

"Better if little is spoken about oneself"

"Give no man the gun and the ammunition to execute you"

"Bridle the tongue and you control the fortress"

"Man is his own executioner. He slowly kills himself by how he lives his life"

"Realism might be hard-hitting now, but the effects might serve you well down the road"

"Sometimes you might get more from something by moving away from it than moving towards it"

"It is during your weak moments when might emerges from the outer world"

"The pain from true love rarely heals"

"Continue to do well, regardless if you are ever recognized for what you do"

"Doing good is an honor, and from such will flow joy, peace, contentment, happiness, and fulfillment that never can be compared"

"As man separates himself from the world, he is apt to experience some physical and emotional resistance"

"Dare to be different from the world and the world will not hesitate to be different from you?"

"Gain is not always in the natural, but also in the spiritual. Upon the realization of this phenomenon, the individual is often better for it"

"One should always keep his purpose for LIVING, forever and foremost in his mind, and more so in his dreams"

"Living is a never ending process for LIFE, and LIFE is the sole foundation for living"

"Live your purpose as if your very life depended upon it. Allow nothing else to dominate the concept of purpose.

Cling to it with all that you are, and if the curtain falls while in route, make every attempt to utter to someone the significance of purpose"

"Seek the one true purpose, and compartmentalize all other competing ones. Only one truly matters, however, it might take some time to arrive at this reality"

"It's not necessary that I have what you have, but the knowledge of such awareness is most important"

"Fight your battles one second at a time"

"When in darkness, you can't find your way"

"The very thing you love is generally your biggest downfall"

"Don't overdo your blessing"

"Recognitions will frequently take many forms, and will be conferred by various means"

"In life there are things that the world is unable to give you. On the other hand, there are things, if the world was able to bestow, you might desire not to accept"

"In observing the behavior of man, a person would be wise to ask, "what's in his mind; what's in his heart; and how is all that expressed to the world"

"Ideas and Ideals are real, regardless if they have materialized"

"Man is often socialized to think of reality as being in a state of matter or substance"

"Sometimes it become mind boggling to perceive gifts without substance"

"The greatest gifts are those without shape, form, or fashion"

"Be very cognizant of what is expressed and to whom the expression is conveyed"

"Doing more, knowing more, and being more is a strength rather than a liability"

"In society, many persons battle against social forces for which they have little or no control. In such instances, the individual is confronted with having to do more, having to know much, much, more than required; and wearing many unnecessary masks to offset forces that permeates the very core of society"

"Sometimes there are accounts that will forever remain unsettled"

"It's not so much whether you achieve a thing or not, but, instead having matured to the degree of indifference"

"Every man must develop a working spiritual philosophy"

"The individual would be better off if he remembered his spiritual philosophy rather than his blues"

"A spiritual philosophy should be the basis of life, therefore, adding depth and breath to his living and insight to his eternal destiny"

"Freedom from something is just as important as freedom to achieve it"

"Seek the high road and you shall not remain a lower road traveler"

"Low level living brings about high level negative consequences"

"Seek spiritual maturity as you would attempt to climb the highest peak, or run the mighty marathon"

"When life become chaotic, center your attention, first and foremost on your intention for existing"

"Remembering your true purpose, and energized about your goals, is a rock from which to stand and a firm declaration of your destiny"

"The gathering of all the apples does not always lead to greater fulfillment. Sometimes, it leads to less contentment"

"Fret not concerning the challenges that plague you"

"When you give hope, you give an essence of LIFE that benefits both the giver and the receiver"

"Life is forever ongoing, always in equilibrium, and always in its entirety"

"The morning light seems brighter, and midnight, a hallmark for closing stages, and the beginning of another"

"The weary traveler construes that he has navigated a million miles; witnessed a thousand sunsets; and prayed a billion prayers"

"Grow me and withdraw not your hand from me; and love me, and I will replicate you in the course of action"

"The corridor to spiritual wisdom is submission to walk the path towards it"

"Reality is relative to explanation and the tendency to observe discriminately"

"We exist is a symbolic milieu where the adorning of symbols is a consistent reminder of experiences foregone"

"Distinguished service is another way of expressing distinguished experiences, lest we be quick to forget"

"Battling over that which has no rule is detrimental to body, mind, and spirit"

"A big plus for self-esteem is choosing not to engage in a war in which the probability of winning is low"

"The more one serves, the more joy is derived from the willingness for having done so"

"There is a spiritual level in which one is not so concerned with who receives the credit"

"In every passing second, one becomes more than he was. Therefore, by measuring the seconds, one can measure his place in time"

"Take advantage of the opportunity to advance, but not to the point when advancement takes the opportunity of you"

"Overcoming the self is not allowing the physical senses to bombard the spiritual essence of the self"

"It becomes very meaningful to achieve a stage in metaphysical evolution when coveted ideas once held no longer have the spotlight"

"Some things we learn to live with; while other things we learn to live without"

"Learning to abstain from fleshly pleasures is a mighty big step towards your spiritual destiny"

"When in darkness, it's not always easy to discern the light regardless of the wattage of the bulb"

"Rest in the joy of what the Lord has already delivered you from; rest in the expectation of your dreams becoming a reality; and rest in the joy of what you have already achieved"

"Every human being has worth, and some individuals have empowered themselves as God to evaluate the worth of another"

"Every individual has immeasurable worth, so pathetic is the idea that much of humanity by its proceedings does not believe it to be so"

"The world's afflictions can only be transformed by afflicted hearts made well"

"You have your gold and silver, I have none. Therefore, I am the better for it"

"No commission, committee, or council can transform social phenomenon of a spiritual origin"

"Some lament about being their brother's keeper, but in keeping your brother, you're keeping yourself"

"Some use the cliché that time heals all scares. Not so if death supersedes the healing of the scares"

"Aging is a benchmark on the footpath to mortality, especially if much of what you once thought to be true suddenly becomes questionable"

"Life is more than what you make it. It's also society granting you permission to do so"

"Emancipation is not an accessible manner of expressing freedom. You are free providing that your freedom does not confine me to slavery"

"It's a momentous occasion when you finally understand the nature of a thing"

"In society there are both written and unwritten laws. Both are perceived as equally significant and their effects are the same"

"Life is a survival process in many ways, but emotional survival is the foundation from which the person stands"

"Racism and any other form of ism is an evil, regardless where it exists, and who is the transporter"

"Racism and other forms of extreme dislike are opportunities for illumination"

"Light requires no prologue, it makes room for itself"

"It's difficult to be content with what you have if your thoughts are on what you yet desire"

"Honor and courage emerge not only from what you do, but from what you choose not to do"

"Not willing to go to war ensures peace of mind; joy of the heart; and future prosperity"

"It's not whether one competes for the prize as it is given the opportunity"

"Your greatest blessing in life is your willingness to give to others that which you'd rather keep for yourself"

"One's greatest blessing produces the greatest joy; and one's greatest joy yields the magnificent testimony"

"Truth has nothing to do with feelings. Truth is simply truth that does not beg for your or my approval"

"It's not what I have achieved that is so sterling, but that which I have chosen not to achieve"

"Inherent within the greatest need is the greatest temptation; and within the greatest temptation is the greatest opportunity"

"Life's greatest treasures are those regarded as insufficient"

"You become what you claim. Claim life and you will live; claim death and death will claim you"

"Life is a journey and each step is a catalyst to heaven or hell"

"Use temptation as an opportunity to do good"

"As a person matures spiritually, one consequence of the process is a reduction in engaging in risky behaviors and activities that contribute to the detriment of a state of peace, joy, and well being. On the other hand, the more immature one is, the greater the risk of involvement in shaky behavior"

"Maximize the meaning of achieved accomplishments, thus minimizing the strain for maximum accomplishment"

"Attention from others is not always a solicitation as it is the draw of the human spirit"

"The Holy writ states that the love of money is the root of all evil. A generalization is expressed that the absence of it has equal consequences"

"Do not be deceived into thinking that because the processes of birth and death are universal that society is totally agreeable"

"Never put your guard down, for the kindest soul can deliver the deadliest blow"

"Watch yourself, again I say, watch yourself"

"A person's greatest critic is often the one you love the most"

"As a way of preserving the self, there are activities that one must refrain from participating"

"Life in and of itself is a series of choices. Choices that are often difficult to make and more so to live"

"Achieving in the natural is good, but in the spirit is better"

"Just as some set out to achieve the gold wreath, so do others seek out the fruit of the spirit"

"Achievement is not always a tangible product"

"A common equalizer for both rich and poor is the process of death"

"Better to reside in a shack with joy and peace than in kingdoms far beyond the realms of reality"

"Great individuals often go unnoticed in a world that defines and chooses"

"Many well known individuals find themselves in miserable situations, while ordinary ones are in worlds beyond their time"

"There are many individuals whose names are emblazoned in the annals of antiquity, yet others whose footprints have walked on the burning sands of time. And the world is a much better place for it"

"That what is desired is not always what is needed, and that what is needed is often what one does not desire"

"Temptation is often a cruel master who relentlessly summons us to unknown perils leading to destruction"

"The beginning of genuineness begins with us"

"What's is in your head will eventually settle in your heart and what's in your heart you give back to the world"

"What's spoken from the lips is a manifestation of what's in the heart"

"Sometimes reflection is made upon where one has been, while at other times it is a process of pondering where one chooses to go"

"Life is a pattern of physical and human emotions traversing a continuum of ups and downs through a medium labeled time"

"Ideas are recurrently cast into expressions fashioned into phraseologies of life and death"

"Ideas, more than mankind, are forever being birthed, yet subject to sudden death without their perpetual resurrection"

"Would you prefer a chest of jewels because of its number, or none because of their meaninglessness?"

"Expressing no to one's desires is not a mark of frailty but of fortitude and insight"

"We walk in solitary; nevertheless, the mass propels itself on a corresponding course"

"You too are a pilgrim, astute to the certainty that passages have not the same span, and that the circumstances of my voyages have not coinciding anticipations"

"Protect the earth for you are from it; protect yourself for you are the earth"

"Weakness is the foundation from which the fortified castle is built"

"Go forth and do good!!!!!!!!!"

"There comes a time when we question our purpose, our being, and the path traveled"

"Pain has a way of showing us the strength we have within"

"Whatever man has come through, it has taken a toll on the natural man, whether the outcomes are positive or negative"

"The making of a human being is an interesting process, but the making of a social being is even more complex"

"For the most part, we are makers of our own reality"

"What is your destiny? Look back in time and see the handwriting on the wall"

"Saying goodbye does not always mean forever"

"I wish you well on your path!"

"So long to those who have gone before? Maybe we will unite on a distant shore. And hello to those of this era, for I am more than willing to be your guidepost to that distant shore"

"I salute you for your achievements and urge you on to greater heights, especially those that have no shape or form"

"Call upon those who offer WORDS that are LIFE everlasting!"

"The morning comes as the night and some of us witness neither"

"Let's love the children of the world while we can and give them the best in us as long as the best we have is best for the children"

"Children are wonderful creations whose sense of innocence is often impaired by those who claim to love them most"

"Love the little children as He did and surely your reward will be all the more"

"Kiss your parents, and love your sisters and brothers. For the time will come when their absence will serve as a reminder of unbearable loss"

"Many of us have lost our parents and God knows what we would give if we could be with them again"

"Tell your dear sisters or brothers who are alive that you love them while the clock ticks on your behalf to an end that is surely to come. For those who have gone on, tell them too!"

"Considered taking the outstretched hand of another instead of drowning in the cesspool of degradation?"

"I can't make you love me. I only pray that one day you will"

"Only you know if you love someone, and only you are a witness to that truth"

"Our hearts cry and our eyes shed tears that no one ever sees but us"

"If you have no love for another, at least have the decency to say so, since what's in the heart comes out with or without your permission"

"Valley's are often low and mountains are far too often steep, and many people have experienced both extremes"

"Tell one another the truth regardless if the interaction leaves you alone"

"Many tears are shed by those alone, and many are shed by those in the company of hundreds"

"Some people will never accept you because you don't fit the mold they have placed you and their ability to keep you there"

"It's one thing to have ignorance and stupidity in your head and another to have both in your heart"

"One individual has the power to give hope to the world long before the race has ended"

"Thank the individual who gives you hope, and bless the ones who cast all manner of doubt against you"

"Moments of gladness cast a shadow, shadows of moments reflect a destiny, and the end of all things reflects them both"

"It's best to walk away from unfamiliar sources who offer so much so soon"

"People have the ability and charm not only to knock down the strong man, but to kill as well"

"We put walls around our hearts to keep people out or to keep what's in the heart from coming out"

"Some people are so good at reading the heart especially when we wear it on our sleeves"

"Life is full of surprises and much, much, more!"

"One thing life is never empty of is: surprises!"

"One person believes he can pull the genie out of the bottle, while another claims that he has already done so. Yet another claims that she/is is the genie"

"Blessings have a way of running you down and sobering you up for the next go round"

"Life generates much stress with no affects on LIFE"

"Every second is an opportunity that is often disregarded"

"Inform your parents how much you love them before the curtain closes and the grave opens"

"We find ourselves in many states of mind. We don't always know which one will guide or deceive us"

"We grow tired of the process and the process probably cries for our exit"

"We find ourselves in many places and in many situations over time"

"Sometimes we find ourselves in many places and many places witness our presence"

"Friends are not the same as associates, but are often regarded as such"

"Friendship is often compared with love. It is often believe to show up and not out"

"Friendship risks being called into action"

"Seldom does friendship remain passive, and if it does, we need to question the concept"

"When challenging times come along, often our friends are not to be found"

"The time comes when we watch in utter despair the bombing of the temple and we fail to say ouch!"

"We do the best we can to maintain the temple even against all odds and the use of synthetics"

"A new time in a familiar setting produces interesting reflections"

"Again, so far away, yet so close in thought from physical reality"

"We hold many special people so dear and close to us, yet knowing that we aren't held in the same regard. For many it doesn't matter, but for a few, it breaks their hearts"

"True love for others is true regardless of circumstances, situations, or mishaps"

"Love does not take kindly to orders and commands"

"Love others for the sake of love, and those who know how to love, will love you too for the sake of love"

"Love forgives, although it might not enjoy the process"

"Say good morning to the world and you might be surprised as to who will respond"

"Sometimes so much is required in performing the simplest things, whereas, rarely is little required in doing the big things"

"Image without heart is vain"

"Sometimes we fall back into the cesspool of life only to realize how much we need rescuing"

"At times we know we are at a place that we rather not be, but the way out appears too difficult at the moment"

"Our lives are stagnant at times and we often wonder when the process to a more fluid reality will come"

"Oftentimes we attempt to be friends to those whose heart for us does no longer love as before"

"Sometimes we must leave things as they are and move towards a better day"

"Life is full of contingencies in which you often have little or no control"

"Our days are linked to what we presently hold first in our hearts and then in our minds"

"Change is only relevant if you think it is"

"Self-change is good, but never to change another"

"Loving will generate suffering of all kinds whether you desire it or not, or whether it is of your doing"

"Spiritual maturity separates a man from his natural self"

"Man never knows when his journey begins or ends"

"The longer you live the more you discover something about yourself and the external world"

"Life is not always a beautiful landscape, neither is it a cesspool"

"To your surprise, some people are likely to be amazed at what you have achieved. Therefore, don't be alarmed at their reactions since you are amazed as well!"

"Knowledge is a cumulative process, but the right knowledge is limited"

"Life might give you the best from a social perspective, but CHRIST gives you more than the best from all perspectives"

"There is something better than the best, but only from the other side of time, place, and space"

"Man was given a helpmate to silence his alienation and to reign in unity"

"Dead ideas can be brought to life with new ones"

"Understanding is a key to greater understanding. Seek it with all your might, and never let it go once you get it"

"Peace. Where does it come from? Better yet, how do you acquire it?"

"Time runs its course in all events regardless of how much we attempt to stall it"

"As said before in a distant place, time is time, and we are guests in its presence"

"Suffering for righteousness is most honorable when we take time to reflect upon the moment"

"There is a way that is unholy, and the remembrance of that concept is relative to LIFE or death"

"Longing for a lost love should not be confused with longing for the art of love"

"Goodness is not always recognized by those we think are most knowledgeable"

"Sometimes, no is the best directive to the saving of a soul"

"Some say home is where the heart is. Others say the heart is not always at home"

"Sadness comes and it goes. Although at times, it returns for a season unwelcomed"

"Laughter is good! Sadness is good! Only if you can learn from it"

"Sometimes you have to sustain a really bad burn to keep from getting a worse one in the future. And at other times, regardless of how often we get burned, a burn remains a burn"

"Some of life's experiences are tough, but if we begin to observe them as positive experiences, then the pain once held begins to diminish"

"What would happen if we began to observe all experiences as opportunities?"

"We come to a place where we have never been before and in our own way wonder how long the visit we must experience"

"Sometimes the way out of a situation is not always forthcoming and we begin to wonder if this is our destiny forevermore"

"Where are those who once informed you of their willingness to be with you always? Now, no trace of them can be found and their presence has left no footprints"

"Man finds himself in the wilderness more than he desires, and oftentimes alone. He proceeds to fight a battle with himself, a battle he is likely to lose"

"Man has nothing to give himself especially when his lips fail to utter a prayer of redemption"

"Man traps himself in an attempt to be savvy and often becomes prey for others to devour in his state of helplessness"

"We continue to cry out to the world, even in silence as if no one hears us"

"How much we wish to turn back the hands of time"

"The clock ticks and there is nothing we can do about it but silence the sound of the ticking"

"The hour is at hand and the second becomes the minute"

"At a particular season in life, we look back in astonishment and wonder where the years have gone"

"All we have is the present and how soon it becomes history"

"The quality of a man's life is in proportion to what he thinks, and what he thinks is more than likely what he gives to the world. It then becomes the responsibility of the world to accept or reject his thinking"

"The day draws to an end in hopes of a new one"

"We come to the end of road and often question where we've been"

"Life is bittersweet and is often hard to swallow"

"Live life to the fullest and never regret one second"

"Everyone has the ability to teach, the question is: what is being taught?"

"We learn so much in so many ways in a given period of time"

"The time comes when we must say goodbye in order to save ourselves"

"Saying goodbye is not always easy; and it never was intended to be so"

"New beginnings are periods of adjustments that are often difficult, challenging, and painful"

"There must never be a break with the holy writ lest you risk losing your way"

"The time comes sooner than later when you stare your destiny in the eyes and wish for borrowed time"

"Time is time and nothing more"

"We reach a point in time when we wonder if we will reach another"

"We don't always know what to do, who to go to, and what to say"

"We cry for help and no one hears us except ourselves"

"Help is not always on the way, nor was it intended"

"Faith is the anchor that we hold on to especially when we are drowning"

"Some cross the line for the first time, whereas, some cross the line for the last time unknowingly"

"Some lines are never to be pondered as an excuse to be crossed"

"Pain is real whether we bring it on ourselves or at the hands of others"

"We do not always like what we have become, but more often than not, we have the capacity to do something about it"

"Give to each human being you best and you will be the better for it"

"One smile has the potential of lifting the heaviest burden"

"We shed tears of vast dimensions and for so many reasons unknown"

"Hearts are pierced in many ways"

"We ache in so many ways and for such an extended period"

"When a crisis emerges, many of our friends scatter like wild fire"

"True friendship is constantly measured in proportion to the severity of a crisis"

"Never be surprised when your need to be heard is met by friends with muffled ears"

"True friendship is rare and is achieved through an honest process over time"

"Those who give a friendly kiss may not always be friendly, if ever"

"Yesterday is gone and will soon be forgotten than remembered"

"The angry man is often more angry with himself than anyone else"

"Anger has many faces in proportion to the person who wears it"

"Even true friends are like the seasons; they at times come and go as they please without our permission"

"Time is briefer today than yesterday and the day before. It is as sand in an hour glass with an appointed destiny"

"Falling in love is a scary thing of which you have no guarantee that the fall will not kill you"

"We look to the future because it is our hope, we glare at the past with tears of joy and sadness because it is life lived, we experience the present because it is our present reality"

"Social living is complex with a tendency to become more so than not"

"We reach to the bottom of the barrel to find nothing there, and we reach to the sky from which we grab on to a star"

"Wisdom is read of in the books of time but often achieved through pain and suffering"

"The sun shines brightly upon us all but the rain is not as lucky"

"Living teaches us many but different things for the benefit of the learner"

"So easy if life taught us its lessons from a book"

"Life's teaching faculty is the many for the few who are willing to be taught"

"Rise up dear friend and take your place among the living and run the race as if your life depended on it!"

"My prayer for you is that the Holy Spirit descends upon you as an eagle after it preys, and warms you as the noon day sun!"

"Other people often give us the best advice except not having walked in our shoes or slept in our beds"

"We look into the lives of others and often swear that we've been where they are, only to conclude that we never came close"

"Events, situations, and circumstances often have a combination of effects on us without our fully understanding their impact"

"Today we are giants and tomorrow we are ants in a colony"

"Our plight can be so grueling in that we wonder if there will be a tomorrow"

"In our lives we wonder if God has gone fishing or on sabbatical"

"Sometimes we ask where is God, and most of the time we don't receive an immediate answer, if any at all"

"Just because God does not work on our time schedule does not mean He's not at work"

"God is everywhere present without fear of being found out!"

"We find ourselves at a place and God only knows where we are"

"When we find ourselves in a lonely place, friends often leave us for a more important task"

"The love of our life does not always come to us in a neat package with a pristine history"

"The truth makes no room for lies but for more truth"

"Our heart will forever hurt over things of which we had no control"

"Please wish the best for all people as they are probably doing the same of which each man is included"

"We hurt most of our days and cry more than we desire"

"The sun rises on us all without anyone's permission"

"We know God is present not so much by feeling his presence but believing in his presence"

"Even in the storm, there is a presence of His being"

"I have loved you for an eternity and have not found you loving me in the slightest manner"

"The sun rises and the sun sets with no one having the eyes to see"

"The tears we cry are ours and ours alone"

"The time finally comes when the union is split and a new beginning emerges"

"We kiss those we love every day, and for many it's our last kiss and our final goodbye"

"I cannot make you love me and I cannot give that which I don't have"

"The band comes off the finger of promise and the finger of promise lays bare in a wasteland"

"I wish you would kiss me one last time and that I felt it had meaning even if it was not so"

"The sun hides it face and the moon rains cups of blood in a world of vast proportions"

"The wolf howls for a time and his demise is near in an uncertain world"

"Take my hand and give me a drink from the fountain of wisdom"

"Help me in this hour because my pain is of great significance"

"See me today and kiss me tenderly because tomorrow is not promised for either of us"

"Kisses are important and much more for those who kiss and those who accepts"

"I have traveled the road and the backpack of memories is tiring. Take it from my weary shoulders for a while. If you choose, you can carry it for me, otherwise, you can lay it down and neither one of us has to touch it forevermore"

"Say hello to the morning since it's not promised to you or me. Greet it as a friend and abide in it before the evening comes"

"I miss you already with incredible pain, knowing that as the sun sets I will be missing you even more in incredible pain"

"Death comes to us in many ways and so does resurrection"

"If I could live some aspects of life over, I would make every attempt to live it with more sincerity. And maybe the outcomes would be better"

"I wish I could make all things right for you; see love in your eyes; and less fear in your disposition"

"I know not your pain, but whatever it is, I would like to remove it, or at least be a band aid"

"Take my yoke upon you for just a season and let me rest for a short time"

"In this hour before the closing of the door, pour out to me the critical issues of your heart"

"The sand in the hour glass has virtually none left and the tears of the clown has almost come to a complete stop"

"If you have ever loved me, show me as no other time. The clock ticks with a rhythm to an end. The morning brings a new sun and the day exclaims a new me. You are a suspect in question either as in the past or in the future. If you love me at all, show me as no other time, for the sand in the hour glass is of a grain and our time together is in judgment"

"Come to me before the moment is too late. Run to me as if your very life depended on my reception. Let the tears flow and the laughter come forward. Kiss my hand and touch my heart once more"

"I have gone to a distant world and the old is history as if for a moment. I cry for you to recognize me as for you, but the you I know is rebelling. Cast not me before or against the curb for the savior of mankind will restore the majesty of my being and uphold me to the God of eternity"

"In all things follow Christ and then, all things will be laced with Christ"

"Christ will show you many things, but you alone must choose"

"Christ will never make you do anything. He gives you choices. The choices don't choose you. You choose them"

"Happy is the man who knows he is on the path of the Holy one"

"Never think that what you have achieved is the ultimate. There is more that has no form or substance"

"Seek the spiritual by which man cannot destroy and time cannot soil"

"Light separates itself from darkness and both cannot coexist"

"When the clouds cover the sun, the sun remains unmoved and unchanged"

"He brings you the truth and the truth remains truth throughout time"

"What do you do with truth if you know not what it is?"

"Some things stare you in the face and the face does not always know it's on stage"

"Chaos leads to chaos and to remedy this phenomenon is to rid the chaos"

"Live unto ME, and I will LIVE unto you. Die unto ME and I will resurrect Myself into you"

"Man is tempted by what he has need of, and what he has need of does not always fit the pattern of morality"

"Man can never say he is alone when he accepts that SPIRIT has forever been with him"

"So nice, so comforting, so complete when the ends of the circle connect"

"Oneness with LIFE is our only and final destiny"

"Time will come when you will desire to say hello to a stranger"

"Going to a fountain that once was sweet brings memories of sweetness that may not be relevant to the hour"

"When the clutter of life has overwhelmed you, find a way back to the philosophy of Christ"

"A person does not always know where a well chosen path may lead"

"So many paths await your footsteps. Which path will you choose and which ones will you avoid?"

"Every context has both its blessings and curses"

"Say hello to each one as you might not have the chance again"

"God is the foundation of all and man is His potential offspring"

"Some things are none of our business and the better off we are when we realize this reality"

"We go our way alone even when there is no one who desires to share the path"

"The clouds turn dark and the sun is nowhere to be found"

"We have our days and the days will have us until there is none left"

"We wonder if where we are at the moment will ever change whether the moment is good or bad"

"We sit at the table wondering what hand to play or what to say about nothing"

"Heartache is something that comes and eventually goes, hoping not to return so soon"

"We have made the confession, now we have to deal with the consequences"

"Let me ride the wave of the unknown surf before I die on a barren battle field"

"Sometimes we desire to run but not sure where to go"

"When all hell breaks loose on you, you cannot always depend on your friends for ice water"

"Sometimes we cry and sometimes we die"

"We don't always know what to do in all situations, but one thing is certain, we can pray"

"We become tired and worn, and sometimes we simply can't go on"

"In our loneliest moment when the human touch has fled our grasp, God, and He alone is our foundation and anchor"

"Take care, maybe we will meet again on a distant shore in another time and place"

"The time comes when goodbyes are final and hello has very little meaning"

"The clock ticks until it stops; the sun rises and sets by its own design; and we die when life no longer can live within us"

"We run the course of life and sometimes we come in second place, if at all"

"We say goodbye to an old friend and kiss the face of a bright eyed baby"

"Many roads should never be travelled and many paths should never have a beginning"

"Paths often become roads that have dead ends or continual openings"

"Altered states are not real and the jokes are on those who fall into such conditions"

"It's not so important that you know who I am, but that you listen well to what I have to say"

"We look with our eyes and become jaded at what we see"

"One should always consider what's at stake before pondering to risk it all"

"If you know what's right, consider the effects for being disobedient"

"Things, conditions, mishaps, and misfortunes all have a way of sucking the winds from our sails"

"Suffering comes, ready or not. But it comes and goes more often than we desire"

"Mature love should never be without its intimacies"

"If my goodness and kindness causes you pain, then by my goodness and kindness set me free"

"Sometimes we can be at the brink of disaster and the Holy One becomes our sole rescuer"

"Reflect on the situation that has engulfed your very being and discover the rich potential awaiting your discovery"

"As the righteous plan is disclosed, so are the potential blessings"

"My God, my God, please have mercy on us. For in so many endeavors we think alone as if your Holy hand has been removed"

"In the midst of this inferno, we feel that all is well and that an essence of YOU is surrounding us"

"Avoid all places of weakness lest you be willing to fall therein"

"New beginnings are often scary and the memory of remaining in hell is devastating"

"Some lines are never meant to be crossed"

"Consider the line before crossing as if your very soul depended on it"

"Once the line is crossed, there is no going back!"

"We stand at the line, wondering if we should cross it. And if we do, what are the consequences, good or bad"

"So many people are attempting to take their lives while so many are desperately hanging on to life"

"Intentionally drowning in the drink never does a person any good. For tomorrow, if he awakes is another day to reconsider the drink"

"Living life is never easy, especially when you have lived long enough to know what living is all about"

"The lights of the temple are dim and the reason for their state is beyond approach"

"The true self is on hold and the emerging one is in its place"

"The emerging self is having its day and the true self waits on time to express reality"

"The world is a world of worlds and a time of times"

"My God, my God, we know you are aware of all our faults and the way we are"

"Forgive our miserable ways oh God! Thus have mercy on our souls that from the very beginning have been immortal"

"Death is a friend and life is the victim of social living"

"Sometimes the path is hard to travel and the lines become blurred into nothingness"

"The ground rules have been set and the boundary cannot be breached lest a penalty is imposed"

"Evaluate the purpose of your going and begin again under a new banner"

"Forgive yourself and begin anew"

"The traveler reaches a certain point and ponders how he got there"

"Take serious not only the cloth but the way of it"

"Sometimes people die so that others might live"

"If the Lord is truly our shepherd, then no one or nothing else should claim such a position in our lives"

"Loving God is the beginning of all things at work in our lives"

"The scale of life is not balanced and just"

"You are just a snapshot in the grand scale of life"

"As the mind is renewed, we become a new creation"

"Truth is not known until you know it, and the power therein is liberating"

"Open windows hardly open by themselves"

"We fail many times and are often unable to regain the position to begin again"

"There comes a time when we must make a decision to move on with our lives, although at times there is resistance to remain parked at the bench"

"Change can be good or bad, and we never know the outcome in the beginning"

"Why consider returning to a place where your funeral has already been preached"

"Life is full of living and living brings with it many challenges and sorrows. Nevertheless, life is full of living regardless if we engage in periods of inactivity"

"Life can also be viewed in how we see it. If we think we see dragons, then dragons are what we see. If we see progress in a negative situation, then progress is what we see. So much is in the eye of the beholder"

"It's not good to be at a place where love is present in words only but not in action"

"Strive to leave your mark on the world as the world has left its mark on you"

"Life does not present itself to each of us in a neat package; it often comes to us in a messy arrangement. What we do with the mess is usually up to us"

"Life's events are usually painful regardless of how we view it"

"How we view situations does not mean that we experience no pain. Some phenomena are painful regardless of how positive the view"

"Sometimes we ask far too little than others are able to give"

"We don't always give what we are able, but what we sometimes think is enough"

"Forcing someone to love you is just force and nothing more"

"Every step is a crossroad or a new beginning. We don't always know the many crossroads we come to or the countless beginnings in our footsteps"

"Desire to begin again in a direction that leads to a more positive outcome. At least make the effort to begin again. Who knows what lies ahead, and who really cares about what has come before. There is nothing we can do to change the past. The only thing we can do is change how we think about it and perhaps work to change ourselves"

"We wish to wake up to a familiar time where there is no conflict, pain, and hard feelings"

"Going the last mile does not mean success. It simply means you traveled the last mile regardless of outcomes"

"We tell the truth and that is all. However, telling the truth is an option that we alone must choose"

"Truth is what we often assert"

"Sometimes we wish for a second or third chance. At times we are given the opportunity, and at other times the door of opportunity is closed"

"Greet every new face with respect and a smile, and strongly affirm each handshake"

"We long to go home, but sometimes there is no home for us to return"

"The door closes and there is no key hole to insert the key"

"We sometimes come to a place and the place knows us not"

"The way is hard and we pray that the road become less of a burden than a persistence weight"

"Sometimes we think our days have come to an end and there is no beginning"

"In the course of advanced living, we have seen much water flow under as well as over the bridge"

"There comes a time when we shed the last tear for the last time"

"When God closes one door he eventually opens another door to the beat of His drum and not to ours"

"Change has come and we are in the beginning of a new season that is often varied, uncomfortable, and lonely"

"In the mix of all that comes with a new season in life, there is an essence of hope and a feeling that everything is going to be ok"

"The journey has now begun, one step at a time"

"The river flows and the sun rises and set in its own fashion"

"We die a little each day and more so under duress"

"We meet the ones we need less than the ones we desire"

"Will your and my life matter is the question we will never know on this side of life"

"Do we reach the end unaware or the beginning unaware?"

"Some ideas must be put to rest so other ones might be resurrected"

"We die each day to the same things and birthed to other things"

"We enable many but pay a price in the process"

"The process to life is a process that we alone only knows"

"We reach for the sky but the sky only recognizes our efforts unto itself"

"Death awaits us all at an appointed time, but seldom are we ever ready for it"

"Love me dearly for I am the dearly beloved"

"We often wish that others made the effort to understand what we are about"

"Although we matter, we are not everything to all people"

"All people are individuals who live their lives in isolated moments one second at a time, and in one second, we can be cast into eternity"

"The vacuum is void unless a righteous soul occupies a place within its confines"

"The moments are rare that you kiss my lips and dive within my being"

"We long for the first time of intimacy and the intimacy of the first time is too long a memory"

"May God see our sins and our shortcomings and evaluate us accordingly with His mercy not according to man"

"Lord, come to us quickly before the morning light and before my strength succumbs to nothingness"

"Loneliness grips us when no one desires us and when we have no destiny beyond the grave"

"Help us dear Lord to help others when they have no strength to withstand the pressure of the falling roof"

"We are the grain of sand in the hour glass, hoping that we are not the last grain to make the final fall"

"The day might be yours and tomorrow accordingly"

"We leave to each other a legacy and a lesson for scrutiny"

"Meet me with a kiss and say goodbye with a salute"

"My words are nothing to the many and truth to those who think they know"

"You take me for granted as the days mellow and the road becomes more familiar. Quite a different process when the days were young and the way more promising"

"Someone waits for us after our death to an old way"

"The breach has been broken and the sorrows of that is forever upon as us as a remedy"

"The way is often hard and the future is not certain for all of us"

"We meet a soul in alliance, but social customs prevent exploration"

"Why does the end of the journey shows our errors held close to the chest?"

"You love me not, yet you remain for the sake of convention"

"We run the race, but often we are scared to death"

"Somewhere in our hearts we know the race is over and that we are the winner or the loser!"

"My words are a memorial to me and an idea for those willing to consider the way"

"Wake up people of the world and make a difference in all aspects of life"

"Do what you can do and forget what others have done or capable of doing"

"The moments are trying and the way unsure, but hold tight to the WORD of the Holy One"

"The door opens to the other world as the door closes to this obscure abyss"

"Beware; the time comes when your brothers and sisters will regard you as having not shared the same womb of a woman"

"We die to ourselves as we give birth to the newness of life"

"Some married people simply can't live as partners or roommates"

"Marriage should never take the place of roommates, nor should roommates pretend as if they are married"

"Some people we never get over, therefore all effort is moot"

"Make sure those who declare "loving you forever" is worthy to utter such a statement since forever is forever"

"Some people look with anticipation to the end as well as to the beginning of life everlasting!"

"Here I am a soul in submission to the beginning"

"Some have tasted of the sweet nectar and have indeed found it most excellent"

"All aspiration is cloaked in the Holy"

"The path is so tiring and we are on our last leg"

"Your love for another is going to be tested. Are you prepared for the test?"

"Do not be surprised if you hear of the mold being broken"

"The eagle is flies above the clouds and the dove flies softly below the timberline"

"A starving man rarely stops eating because of his morality"

"Even in our sins, we sense there is hope of salvation"

"I have known you not, yet your knowledge of me has always been paramount as to no other"

"Some people will bring to others restoration, even if it's just for the moment"

"The drowning man does not care whose hands that pulls him from the drink"

"Starvation is real other than the absence of food to sustain the body"

"We hold allegiance to those who saves us from whatever the calamity might be"

"You never cut off the hand that feeds you no more than killing the messenger who delivers the message of HOPE"

"Somewhere is time we meet someone who we connect with on so many dimensions, and yet because of circumstances we are reluctant to clear the cobwebs that would allow our being with them. This often leads to regrets and sadness of the soul"

"We are ourselves and yet we are despised because who we are is not what others desire us to be or simply because we exist"

"The true measure of an individual is inherent in his being"

"A man with an evil heart is walking a tightrope to self destruction"

"Often we fail the tests of life only to realize that through failing the tests we become better prepared to pass those awaiting us"

"It's one thing to know the way and another to understand it. By all means seek to understand the way"

"The wind blows from many directions so as people who enters and exits our world"

"As breath leaves the temple, so do I leave you too"

"Age cometh without your permission and death is the mighty capstone"

"Take the arrow from the wounded and banish the evil spirit from amidst the innocence"

"Every day is one of rebirth relative to our ideas, thoughts, and actions"

"In our quest of faith, sometimes we wonder if God has gone on vacation"

"Love is a powerful force; therefore, never underestimate its capability in a variety of directions"

"Some days we find our way, and other days we lose sight of the vision"

"The time comes for all things to end. And rarely are we prepared to be a witness"

"Many mountains as these have we climbed, but to our surprise this one appears quite challenging"

"The times comes when decisions must be made with or without our best judgment"

"Somehow amidst the confusion, pain, and sadness, a small voice speaks to us with comfort and cheer"

"The seasons come and they go, but memories remain constant as the day and the night"

"Give thanks to those who have brought you joy and to those who bring a promise"

"Thanks for the kiss of confidence and for your embrace as no other"

"If we only experience true love for once in our lives and just for a moment, then that is enough since true love comes around once and awhile"

"It takes so much courage to walk away from what you desire, especially if it's there awaiting your acceptance without limitations"

"We come to a point when we wonder if life is really worth the price we are paying"

"There seems to be a season that we recognize as significant"

"The end draws near and a new one is on the horizon"

"We need to say good-bye to a time past and look with renewed vigor toward tomorrow"

"We take to future our history and that history become a measuring rod for future events"

"We stand at the crossroads each second. Sometimes we stand too long and at other times we move too quickly"

"There are so many ways of failing with the intent of doing right"

"We come to many places in our lives and find out that we have come nowhere"

"We understand little if nothing at all"

"We at times want to give all we have, but realize we have nothing to give"

"Man is forever falling on his face and forever seldom getting up"

"We come to the end and realize the end is very real"

"Often times we think we have it all together, only to realize we never did"

"Never cross the line and you will never have to remember having done so"

"Once you cross the line you can never undo what has been done"

"We thank those whose kindness is forever remembered"

"The pathway to the kingdom is becoming less cluttered and the certainty for some of us getting there is more assured"

"We are not always happy to see some people leave our lives, but neither are we pleased for them to remain"

"Sometimes it appears as if there is no gas in the engine, while at other times the engine is running with no place to go"

"The flesh is never satisfied and the pursuit to fulfill its desire is always challenging and costly"

"Never leave a good way just to prove the difference"

"Healthy fear at the moment is not thought of in such a manner"

"Brothers and sisters on your way, I trust all is well with you and that you are well with God"

"Finding fault in another lends itself to others finding fault with you, thus leading to a vicious circle"

"Sometimes the storms of life kill, and at other times they become our friends"

"Spending time alone can be a lonely, scary, and shocking experience if time alone is your enemy"

"Every person should seek the silence for in its presence are moments for golden reflection"

"The sun rises before us all and bows out of sight without our consent"

"Sometimes we fail to say or do the right thing at the appropriate time. At other times we fail to do anything at all"

"Sometimes it's time to go and at other times it's time to stay. Oftentimes we know not when to go or when to stay"

"It's difficult to leave someone you love when leaving is the best path to take for all concerned"

"Although we make claim to ourselves, we are bought with a price, and if we are bought with a price, someone beyond ourselves made the purchase"

"Knowing that God is with us is more than feeling that He is with us since feelings change as the seasons"

"Some of us are beyond the gateway of our season in many respects and the tests and trials of life roll in and

roll on. We often come to the resolution that through the tests and trails we are better vessels than before"

"Going the distance and lacking the memory from whence we came is a process we might have to endure"

"We often get tired of the way things are and yet too afraid to make an exit"

"Spirit has LIFE eternal and those to whom it is given is consumed by it forever more"

"Having more does not always mean having happiness"

"Sometimes having less can bring about contentment and fulfillment"

"One can always become creative whether they have more or less"

"If you have more of something, why settle for less than what you have"

"Be still, quiet the temple, and listen to the breeze that sings a melody to the soul"

"Liking an individual is not the same as knowing him or her, and knowing the individual is a good indicator whether you truly like the individual in question"

"How often do we think of those who broke our hearts, and how often do we deny our role in the process"

"Wisdom comes not so much from reading and discourse, but from the tests and trials of a weary life"

"Reflect on the past, appreciate the present, and ponder the future"

"Time spent alone is a good thing. For out of the process come nuggets of gold for the soul"

"Yesterday is gone and is now history. Today is all we have in anticipation for tomorrow"

"Tomorrow is not promised and neither is the all too soon second"

"Another day and the beauty of the sun shine upon all"

"Honesty is as grapes of gold glittering in the rays of a heavenly sun"

"Kiss my lips before I die, and hold my hand lest I fall"

"Walk with me the extra mile and see if we are the better for it"

"Saying goodbye can be for a moment and not a lifetime. In some instances, a moment is a lifetime"

"God gives us dreams and far too often we beg relentlessly for overwhelming signs"

"The morning comes with its freshness for a new day. Join hands with the morning and embrace what it has to offer"

"Evening falls because of its season, we often fall because of compelling negative choices"

"Resurrect the mind and the body will prosper"

"Destroy the mind and the body will follow suite"

"Die to self and LIFE is the consequences"

"In all thy getting, seek true understanding since understanding is relative individuals, societies, and nations"

"Understanding, like common sense is relative. What one person understands might be in total opposition to another. And what is common sense to one is foolish to another. It's amazing that wars have been fought and millions have died because of our understanding and common sense notions of some phenomena"

"How do we know the truth from fable? Or does it really matter to you?"

"There is not a remedy for everything, only a prayer"

"Knowing and loving you is not always an indication of trusting and believing in you"

"Trust is fragile, so handle it carefully. Once broken, it's unlikely subject to repair"

"People are not always predictable and neither are our lives"

"So many people, so many ideas, so many souls, so many"

"Time never takes a vacation, the sun always shines, and the moon always casts its shadow"

"Children are innocent and on their way toward an unknown mountain of ignorance called the world"

"Children in all their innocence are the master teacher whose instructions are often ignored as child's play"

"If love cannot have all of love, then love would rather risk having love"

"Some people we see just for a moment and other people we can't get rid of"

"Thinking and feeling are two separate phenomenons. Are you guided by what you think or what you feel?"

"Maturity is increments of experiences methodologically stretched on the plane of time"

"Maturity is a never ending process that we often repeat to reach full blossom"

"Maturity is often viewed as the school of life and time is the professor who is relentlessly on the job"

"Maturity is sometimes difficult to judge, especially when we thought we had come through a certain phase suddenly and successfully"

"We often judge others as weak when in reality they are strong"

"Strength is not always determined by the weight we can lift but by the courage to say "I'm sorry" or to ask for forgiveness"

"Every individual has his strengths and far too often his weaknesses"

"When you truly love someone, then you truly love them, and there is nothing else to be said about it except that you truly love them"

"It's difficult to lie about what you know is the truth"

"Another day has been granted to us and how it ends depends upon our choices"

"Say hello to those you admire and salute those at the crossroads"

"Today might be your day in the sun and maybe tomorrow will be mine"

"The hour is near when so much comes to an end, and a new beginning is birthed out of chaos, and the minds and hearts are mourning their demise"

"The fight has begun with little to fight with and little to win"

"For many, love left a long time ago and we are left wondering if love was there from the outset"

"Saying goodbye is easy for some, and mere hell for others regardless of whom is the victim or perpetrator"

"A heart has the capacity to recover from its break, and a mind has the ability to assist in the healing process"

"Make sure you find the right somebody and not just anybody"

"God, where are you in the midst of this raging storm. Wait! I hear God say, "I am in the midst of the storm"

"We fail each other many times, and sometimes we fall in the failure and never recover"

"Forgiveness is not always easy and it may not always be expressed, especially in the moment"

"Somewhere in time I will see you again. And maybe we will be better to and for each other"

"Hello to you today and goodbye to you tomorrow"

"After awhile we come to the conclusion that other people have no place for us in their world. Oftentimes we concur that not being in their world is best for all concerned"

"We wish we could make others love us, however, we usually come to realize that forcing someone to do something that is not from the heart is more fictional than real"

"Having no place for me in your heart does not always mean that I have no place for you"

"The heart does not take orders very well. It usually is the guiding spirit of the temple and dictates to us the orders of the day"

"Life goes on without the need of our presence"

"Never confuse an individual's confidence as arrogance. Maybe it's your arrogance that's getting in the way of your clarity of mind"

"What does love mean to the soul who confesses it but never shows it. More importantly, what does such love mean to the recipient that does not result in action?"

"Sometimes we dread tomorrow since we aren't sure what tomorrow will bring"

"So many people are fighting to stay alive, yet so many people are wishing to die"

"The deed has been done and the pain is ever before us"

"We cry to ourselves regardless of how much or how little we choose to admit the process"

"Tears are tears; pain is pain; and there's enough to go around for us all"

"We see the evening coming and yet we do nothing in preparation for it"

"Sad hearts do unite if just for a moment. Such a moment in time can mean the world to those who are suffering"

"We have committed sins; now we are remorseful; we begin to seek forgiveness from the Holy One; we find forgiveness from both God and ourselves; and now we pray that we survive the aftermath of the sin"

"Wake up dear one and think of me as I have awaken and am thinking of you"

"In the moment of today we wonder about those we love who for whatever reason loves us not"

"We dream dreams of a distant time when life was perceived as good. But time has run its course and we now ponder about such a time and wonder just how good it really was"

"Death happens in so many ways and unto so many things that we forget the many funerals"

"We often take our varied selves to the fountains of life and sip the drink while we have the time"

"The hunter emerges from the dark forest forever changed"

"There comes a time when we must begin again. If that means changing locations, friends, and ideologies, then that is what we must do"

"Sometimes we kiss the ones we love for the last time and say goodbye too often before the dawn"

"Time comes in all our lives when we should have taken a path less traveled"

"If we could live life all over again, I suspect we would live it in the same manner or not live it at all"

"The wind blows against our faces, but the sun dries our bleeding hearts"

"The path we trod has been hell, but a new day is emerging and there is hope as never before"

"We are usually our own worst enemy and fear is the culprit that has taken up resident"

"Seek forgiveness from those you have harmed, and right the wrongs to those who will allow you. Otherwise, give it to the Holy One"

"Look at each individual and realize that life has taken its toll on both mind and body"

"The day comes to an end and the end is birthed as a new day"

"Some have been to the mountaintop and others have decided to stay for a season"

"The well is dry and the mountain stream has lost its force"

"Babies certainly cry for sustenance and old men die from too much of it"

"The pathway to life is scary unto you have a discovery from the Holy One!"

"This moment we are alive and the next we are dead, yet in the moment we live elsewhere in some dimension"

"Reach out to all men and women as some are probably reaching out to you"

"We all at times feel the urgency to run the race more diligently, but often we have little or no gas in the tank"

"Be gentle with each creature as you would like others to be with you"

"The weathered hands have had their season, and the tired feet have made plain their path"

"Walk with me in this hour for my heart is breaking and death is at work in me as never before"

"Touch my face gently and let me know that I am alive once more before the dawn"

"Yesterday is gone and today is all we currently have"

"History is made with every passing second, and the events within these fleeting seconds have their story that cannot be replicated"

"The future is bright if we make it so, and the sadness of yesterday is further understood with humility"

"We cross many mountains in the course of life and probably more rivers, creeks and streams. The acid test is not in the crossing, but the attitude and the manner in which we choose in the crossing process"

"Forgiveness is needed by all and should be practiced more often than spoken"

"Come down from the mountain and rest for a season for the journey will begin all too soon as if in the morning"

"The fields of our lives need to be plowed and cultivated often by those who know us not"

"The games are over and the tests of life are upon us"

"The morning has come to light and another day is upon us. What we do today depends upon the choices we make. Let's make good choices that will positively affect the world"

"Often times, new beginnings are painful and scary and we detest having to experience them"

"Each of us is a significant blessing to the world. We need to believe that each of us will come into the full revelation of this observation. By doing so, we will see each other in a different light and dispel the darkness that many of us hold for mere individuals"

"Each of us can be a blessing or a curse to the world. Which do you choose to be is in your hands"

"Sometimes we lament and say "I have nothing to give," What about giving your smile to others? Smiling is contagious and when you smile there is a tendency that you feel better, even for the moment. Go forth my friend and give to the world, and in time, if not immediately, the world will smile with you"

"It's so very difficult to give up the people we love, especially those who love us not"

"Saying good bye is such a difficult thing to do, especially for those who love so deeply"

"The pain from loss is a terrible predicament, a situation that we would rather not fall in so soon, If ever"

"The concept that time heals every scar is not always true; especially if we transition before the healing"

"Out of the heart come so many things"

"The day has come and a new journey is upon us"

"We stand at the path and say goodbye forever more"

"It becomes a sad commentary when we aren't able to express what we profess"

"Saying you love someone isn't enough, you must show them"

"If you confess love for another, what are the issues in expressing it?"

"Express what you confess to someone, otherwise write them a letter"

"Some people can never get it together to express what's in their heart. Could it be there was nothing to express from the outset?"

"What can one give when there is nothing to give?"

"Home is where the heart is, but if there is no home, there is no heart"

"We often desire to go to a safe place to dwell and rest for awhile. The challenge is in finding a safe place"

"Some people ache to return home, but there is not always a grand reception"

"On the one hand never give up too soon, and on the other hand, don't wait too long in letting go"

"We all will suffer sooner or later, as suffering is a major part of life"

"If your time has come and gone, be ready for the next adventure"

"So many smiling faces, yet so many hurt unknown"

"Change is hardly easy, but it's necessary in the grand scheme of things"

"Broken love is hardly forgotten long after the show is over"

"Enough pain helps us connect to the one great Source"

"Oftentimes when we ask God for strength, He usually places us in situations or conditions that require us to be strong"

"I know not where your paths have led you. I only know that perhaps I am in your way"

"Let us reason out our differences so that we can plant the spring crops and reap a bounty of blessings in the fall"

"We ponder the past, knowing that we can't go back and undo anything. All we can do is ponder the past and perhaps learn from it"

"My heart cries for all humanity to love one another"

"The time comes when we no longer voice sentiments of praise and love another"

"Love without action is love only in voice"

"The time comes when all is said and done"

"We all remember a time when we thought what was would never be what it has become"

"The dye has been cut and the cut is forever its form and never to return as it once was"

"Our minds have the tendency to drift on the past and the past is in its form and shape to remain in its form and shape"

"Since your lips are forever sealed, let not thy soul follow suit"

"Death comes in many ways and we are never prepared for it"

"The season's crop is ready for picking and the light of the moon has shown forth for your direction"

"The day comes when we rejoice and the day comes when we can't help but mourn and cry without desiring to do so"

"Often we wonder if we have made the right decision in doing what we thought was the right thing to do"

'We hardly say we have cried for the last time when we have been crying all our lives"

"We wonder at times where they are who said they would never leave us"

"We are often treated as those we never were in the eyes of the dead who lives"

"There are no more kisses, no more hugs, no more laughter, and no more of anything. There is no more of no more"

"The die has been cast; the ribbon has been cut; and a toast lifted to the world"

"The journey has begun more than a step at a time, but a frantic pace"

"I am here, but not alone. You are where you are, and you too are not alone"

"The rain falls and the snow eventually melts, but the wind blows its breath on both the living and the dead"

"The journey of life is just that, a journey. A journey of no known ending"

"When reality is fully recognized, a new journey begins to emerge"

"As man creates his social world, so does he creates his problems"

"When we cross the line, we sooner or later come to realize that though we win or lose in the process, it's all part of our destiny"

"We run the race of life not really knowing if we will win or lose. Nevertheless, we run the race"

"We lean on a time that's wasn't real and wonder how to make it go away"

"We struggle with or against something. At the time of our struggle, we are not always certain of the outcome. The more intense the struggle, the more we consider with intensity how we will prevail"

"So many times we wish for yesterday, yet realize that yesterday is gone"

"If we could make amends for past actions, we probably would at the cost of not being so popular"

"Make every attempt not to sin as you once did"

"Today is a new day and what we do with it is up to us"

"Each individual has been given a number of years, a number of months, a number of weeks, a number of days, a number of hours, and a number of seconds to do as he wills"

"The time comes when your joy will overcome you and leave you in a state of ecstasy!"

"Again, I reach my hand to you, here I am"

"The day finally arrives when the flood gates are open and we are washed out to sea with hopes of being rescued"

"Sometime, we are put in a situation that requires us to love the person who hates us to the point of killing us without remorse"

"Joy comes from within and becomes a most precious gem that only you come to discover"

"As time runs its course, we must realize that people do too"

"There is an answer to the problem we face and a mystery often surrounds its resolution"

"Sometimes we have nothing to say of value to anyone or about anything"

"We come to a point in our lives when all what we value and believe is put to the test"

"Sometimes the drama in our lives is so hectic that we play the part of puppet and puppeteer"

"The sun shine brightly on the earth and another day begins anew"

"As we draw near in a season, we begin to look more deeply than before"

"Each of us has many seasons in many contexts. Some are beginning as others are ending. Others are ending as some are beginning. Some are waiting to be born"

"Do well to all for a sense of fulfillment and wellbeing"

"The sun does set and eventually the moon rises"

"We remember the old times, but the old times do not remember us since it is history"

"Wish those you once knew, God's best, and maybe they are wishing you the same"

"So many people are hanging on to life while so many are letting go"

"The price we pay for love and the price we pay without it"

"So many wrongs we would right if only we could do it over again"

"We come to a place and fully realize that we have not been insightful in the choices we have made and the direction we are traveling"

"Seek the spirit of peace in all things. A peace no one can give you and a peace no one can take from you"

"We wish for yesterday concerning private matters and look forward to a renewed tomorrow"

"Live today as if it were the last day of your life"

"We don't always do our best, although we are quick to profess our aggressive efforts"

"We wish for a new beginning, especially when we have messed up our lives and the lives of others"

"Perseverance is a crucial element in any endeavor and we are likely to miss our goals without its application"

"The night comes and the dawn might be too long in coming"

"Rare is the moment when we fail to look back from whence we came"

"The pathway welcomes us all regardless of what we encounter along the way"

"Goals are more attainable when we have seen with clarity the vision"

"Morning is often a refresher when the night has been a tiresome journey"

"Never discount the positives that might emerge from difficulties"

"The day comes and the night finds its place"

"The road behind us is just that – behind us. We can't go back one inch"

"Our pain from living and lying can run deeper than any ocean and cut completely to the bone without fail"

"We come to a place and often think we have arrived at our appointed destiny"

"Today shadows yesterday only if we allow it"

"We come to a place and wonder if we are suppose to be here"

"We reach a point when we are no longer able to hang on, but afraid to let go with little or no choice but to let go"

"The day comes when all that has been planned is put to sunder"

"What will tomorrow be like and what role will we play in making it a reality?"

"The thoughts of yesterday lingers on, and what a relief if we could escape the pain"

"Summer comes to an end and autumn gives a hearty hello"

"The time comes and our very souls are at attention"

"We pass the place of commons and blow a kiss for what once were"

"Hello and Hello again without a response from anyone"

"We give so many signals about so many things that we forget what signals were conveyed and to whom"

"Carry the torch of Life so no one can lose sight of the path"

"All paths need to be seen with clarity"

"Some things we are able to let go with ease, other things take a little more time for which we are often criticized"

"Each of us has something significant to say and each of us has something of worth to give. Have you discovered what it is you want to convey? Have you discovered what it is you have to give? It is up to you and you alone"

"Count your blessings every day and see how quickly the blues go away"

"Silence is golden only if we can be silent"

"We reach a point when we give up hope, and hope says goodbye, perhaps for all time"

"Giving your best is most admirable, but sometimes, it is not enough to win the day. Nevertheless, always give your best regardless of the outcome"

"The wild wolf runs with the gentle sheep and both understands the other"

"We tire quite often from struggle and struggle often takes its place as well as its position"

"We would rather hide than fight when we have no more fight in us"

"Some people see strength within us when we see nothing but desperation disguised as strength"

"We fight the good fight or fight a good shadow"

"The temple is out of sorts and the windows need cleaning"

"The end is in sight and the journey has been good"

"The body is the temple and the temple has been tested beyond belief"

"We need to listen more than we speak, and speak when what we have to say is of importance"

"Friendship is golden, so handle with care"

"Time is taking its toll on the few as well as on the many"

"The day is as short or as long as we think it to be"

"The wind is as time to all mankind. It does not prejudice nor discriminate against any"

"Some practices add health and life to our mortal bodies, while other practices contribute much quickly to our dying"

"Appreciate today because it might be all you have as a basis for tomorrow"

"The past is history as a cemetery is to those who once lived"

"Life is really important and should be viewed in such a manner. If you think this is a fleeting assertion, ask those whose lives hang in the balance and see what their reply is"

"Walk tall this present second as you have always been most worthy"

"The sun will shine again and the wind will blow gently on your being"

"Much of how today turns out depends upon the choices we make or have made"

"Of all your choices, choose to live a Spirit filled life with emphasis on Christ"

"Again, we extend the hand, not knowing who might reach for it"

"The window closes either by itself or with the assistance of others known or unknown"

"The clock continues to tick and history is made with each passing second"

"History is made as each second gives way without its permission to the past"

"The present is measured in seconds as history is the result of fleeting present seconds too minute to capture"

"We come to the end of things and the beginning of other things regardless of being ready or not"

"The winds have swept the regions of the earth and they still are at their work"

"Tears continue to run their course and we hope that we are the better for the process"

"We have made our choices and are not better off than before. As a matter of fact, we are worse than before"

"We come to the valley of the shadow of death so many times that we wonder in amazement our still being alive"

"We have cried too much and have laughed too little about nothing"

"The sun shines brightly in its appearance. It's a splendid thing that it never reflects the heart of mankind. Otherwise there would be no light"

"A hug from an innocent child; the warmth of a scruffy hound dog; the warm embrace of an elderly soul; a soft, gentle kiss in a starry sky; and a salty tear upon our departure. So is the attributes of life"

"We run the race of life at different speeds depending upon our state of mind and the sense of urgency"

"Decisions to deny the self of indulgences are never easy"

"Life is full of occasions either to rise or to fall"

"The test of character is always in the daily decisions that we make"

"Rise up from your bed and listen to the higher calling"

"The day comes to an end, and where are we at the moment"

"Yesterday has come and gone. Are we better or worse? That's the ultimate questions"

"Sometimes we must come to the conclusion that we have done all we could do, regardless if we think we could have done more. The reality is that you did what you could do"

"The weight of the world is not on our shoulders, but at times it certainly feels like it"

"Relating to the world is not easy, especially when you are thought of from the outset as less than human"

"Relationships are not easy, even the best of them"

"Relationships are dichotomous in that two must play the game"

"The individual alone cannot master the relationship since another player has equal opportunity"

"Relationships require a tremendous amount of work, discipline, and fortitude. Are you up to the challenge?"

"If you have failed in a relationship, are you the seed for its failure, or the blessing for a new beginning?"

"Some relationships can be salvaged while others need to remain dead"

"If good relationships are not properly managed, then the risk of destruction is imminent"

"Death is close to life and life is close to death. What an interesting cycle"

"We live and sooner or later we die. We die and no one truly knows how we lived or how we learned to live"

"A new time awaits the world in a second. So does the past!"

"We come and we go. We just come and we go. Somewhere, if anywhere, we come and we go"

"The wind blows without permission. And those in its path feel its touch without our permission"

"Memories are there for remembering, only if we are able to recall them"

"More than once have we wondered if we have come to the end of life's road?"

"The day is upon us and the future of it is unknown"

"Some things you never forget how to do; others things you never learn how"

"We come to the end of the road and stand at the gate. Often wishing we could return along the way and make amends to those whose heart we have offended"

"Faith is what we hold on to long before the sun has lost it shine and the moon its shadow"

"Most of our conversation with the world is secular and not spiritual in nature. One of the many reasons is that secular society has a difficult time interpreting spiritual language"

"Practice the mind of Christ and we will become more like Christ"

"At times we are shown the way and at other times we could care less"

"We grow our children in proportion to what we sow into their lives"

"The seeds of greatness are not always within or without"

"We fight the good fight not always winning or losing the battle"

"The sword is not always sharp; nevertheless, it remains a sword"

"The WORD is spoken never knowing if anyone is listening"

"We laugh and we cry in hopes for a better tomorrow"

"We tire to a point of fainting in hopes that we will revive"

"Keep one foot ahead of the other and maybe you will reach your destination. What is your destination?"

"At times we envy what others appear to have, therefore, not really knowing what they truly have"

"Life is a puzzle with many pieces with many hands attempting to complete the picture of life"

"Every day brings a fresh, new way of thinking and observing the world in which we live"

The Old Man

The old man sits on the grassy hill....
Wondering if he should swallow the deadly pill...

The sun hides its face behind a mountain of gray clouds...
As the old man prays to God out loud...

God responds, "I am the way"...
And the old man utters, "You have made my day..."

The Battered Wolf

The battered wolf howls relentlessly in the cold, frigid night...
Trying desperately to arouse anyone in sight...

He limps slowly from a hostile fight...
And howls that much more of his desperate plight...

His limp succumbs to a bombastic fall...
As he lies dying against the canyon wall.

The Flowing River

A river flows from a pair of eyes...

Consistent with the trail of lies...

The face is now contorted with pain...

And there is no evidence of gain...

Tears of Anguish

I cried tears of anguish all last night...

As I gave thought to our challenging plight...

I love you dearly as no other...

As they were not really worth bothering...

I give you my heart....

To be a part...

Of this great love...

As pure as a dove...

The Closed Door

The door is now forever closed....

Much as how we often preferred....

I will perhaps see you on the other side...

If we turn not against the tide...

You Say You Love Me, Is It So?

You say you love me, is it so?

Then I anticipate a welcoming glow...

Instead I see a solemn face...

As tight and as rigid as a leather lace...

You say you love me, is it so?

Then make it special for it to become so.

The Man in the Mist

I saw in the mist a figure of a man...

I never gave any thought whether he had a plan...

He walked toward me in a frantic pace...

As I turned to run I tripped and fell on my face...

He stood over me in my state of fear...

Just to let me know he was near...

He said to me, "Give me your hand my dear"...

As I have been with you far and near...

To keep you safe in this land of fear...

The Inner Man

The inner man...

Has all the plans...

The inner man...

Has the upper hand...

The inner man...

Like grains of sand...

The inner man...

Is all over the land

Time

Time in the sun...

Just having some fun...

Time in the rain...

Yet proving I'm sane...

Time in the snow...

When the heart is feeling low...

Time in my tears...

Awaiting Christ to appear...

Christ

Christ at the dawn of morning...

Is all the adorning...

Christ at noon...

He's never too soon...

Christ in the evening...

What a welcoming seasoning...

Lips of Death

I allowed her to kiss me with her lips of death...

Knowing beforehand I might lose my breath...

Her passion enveloped me as the noon day sun...

And I spoke as a mad man of how much fun...

I cried out to God against my act of scorn...

For His wrath came down on me as if blown from a kudu horn...

And God opened the heavens with His forgiving rain...

And relieved my soul from its everlasting pain.

www.ingramcontent.com/pod-product-compliance
Lightning Source LLC
Chambersburg PA
CBHW020509290526
45786CB00002B/530